With much love
On your journey
Sandy!
♡ Cori

Choosing a Vibrant Life

CORI ELLINGSON

This material has been written and published solely for educational purposes. The author and the publisher shall have neither liability nor responsibility to any person or entity with respect to any loss, damage, or injury caused or alleged to be caused directly or indirectly by the information contained in this book.

The author of this book does not dispense medical advice or prescribe the use of any technique as a form of treatment for physical, emotional, or medical problems without the advice of a physician, either directly or indirectly. The intent of the author is only to offer information of a general nature to help the reader in the quest for a vibrant life. In the event the reader uses any of the information in this book for self or others, the author and the publisher assume no responsibility for the reader's actions.

This book and its contents are not intended to diagnose, treat, or cure any infection, injury, or illness, or prevent any disease.

ISBN 978-0-9878774-2-0

If you would like to publish sections of this book, please contact the publisher for permission.

Published by:
Cori Ellingson
PO Box 20017
Duncan, BC
V9L 5H1
cori_ellingson@hotmail.com

Editing by Carole Audet. Cover photo by Kim Yanick Portraits. Cover design and typesetting by Euan Monaghan.

Dedication

To all courageous pioneers,
ready to embrace
the infinite possibilities
opening
before our very eyes,
in this precious time to be alive.

Contents

Foreword

When my mom asked me to write a foreword, I felt excited as this book will open her vast knowledge to a wider audience. I feel incredibly fortunate to have her as my guide. She has taught me to question the mainstream approach to living, and examine the ways society has been led astray. The journey of inquiry to find the truth behind the façade and decide how to proceed can be challenging. The contents of this book are a distilled version of the gems my mom unearthed during her 60 years of digging into living life more vibrantly.

Our whole family has been pioneers on the path of learning about health and wellness for more than 40 years. That kind of dedication to any type of venture is sure to bring success when you consistently walk your talk. We must embody and practice our ideas before we share them. Mom is one of the most happy, healthy, and vibrant people that I know, and anyone who has met her would agree.

In the early 1970s, my Uncle Donon, Mom's eldest brother, made the choice to leave his teaching career and before long had opened a vegetarian restaurant. Unfortunately, it was too far ahead of its time and closed after one year. However, with help from the family, Uncle Donon went on to start, own, and operate five health food stores in Vancouver, British Columbia. He served as President of the Canadian Health Food Association from 1974 to 1977. As a leading edge thinker and advocate for personal choice and freedom, he made great strides in the industry using his gifts of passionate writing and speaking.

By the time I came into the picture in 1984, our family already had 25 years worth of knowledge about natural medicine and its awesome potential. Through her own research and intuition, Mom chose not to vaccinate me that year, a very radical decision in our little farming community. It was not easy to stay strong amidst family members' fear for my safety. However, I am incredibly grateful for the conviction of her beliefs since I've consistently been one of the healthiest of all my peers.

It is with great pleasure and honor that I am able to share some of my direct interaction with the author of this book. To talk about urine therapy, fasting, juicing, mushrooms, physical-emotional connection, ayahuasca, breath work, and quantum healing all before lunch wouldn't be out of the question with Mom.

I can remember her telling me at a young age to *ask* the aloe vera plant I was about to harvest, "Which leaf wants to help my body with the healing it needs?" I aced a karate board break by the time I was ten, symbolically breaking through challenges I wanted to overcome. At age twelve, I worked with a group to build a sweat lodge where we later enjoyed many healing ceremonies, connecting with the earth and elements, in ways unheard of for most kids my age. At sixteen, I successfully walked across hot coals representing my greatest fears during a fire walk, opening me to my huge potential. By eighteen, my natural ability to speed up the healing process of the human form by directing my energy was ignited. Mom and a friend shared their Reiki knowledge with my sister and me, a gift that will last the rest of my life.

Mom has strived to inspire countless people to live a better life with her knowledge, skills, and wisdom. Some of her practices include: NLP, Reiki and other energy healing modalities, drumming and chanting circles, along with workshops to enhance personal growth including those that involve shamanic practices. She taught vegetarian and vegan cooking classes and hosted Awakening the Dreamer symposiums. She leads sacred cacao and full moon fire ceremonies internationally. I want to continue her legacy of sharing honestly from the heart with all who cross my path.

Mom taught me from an early age to take responsibility for my choices since we all have the power to radically change our own lives. When I was able to truthfully evaluate my choices, that honest shift opened me to choose again, in alignment with the path I truly wanted. No one else could make sense of my experiences and help me navigate the emotional roller coaster that life can be. The most powerful thing I've learned from Mom is the inspiration to question normal ways of living and explore the road less traveled to uncover what else is possible. It's not always easy being different; however, being authentic has brought me satisfaction and success.

Mom's devotion continues to inspire me to stay true to my path in life, unaffected by what others think. It's crucial we each take time to assess the ground we stand upon, choose to deconstruct what isn't working, and build a new foundation that will take us toward the future we wish to see.

As humans we have an exquisite opportunity to shape the world around us by examining and shifting the world inside of us. Our thoughts, beliefs, and emotions are incredibly important to our sustained well-being. It's an exciting time to be alive and even better now that this book is in your hands.

Tanner Ellingson
Inspired Wellness Consultant
Reiki Master Teacher
Yoga Teacher

Acknowledgments

It takes a whole village to
raise a child and
several villages to birth
and bring a book to completion.
With heartfelt gratitude to many dear friends and
family members in villages around the world.
Together our love, inspiration, and support
as we each do our part will catalyze a
new and gentle world of unity
where all can thrive.
Gratitude to Junie Swadron,
for brilliant, intuitive guidance and friendship.
Much gratitude to my friend Nola Watson,
my laughter buddy and fun-loving sounding board.
Thanks for being there through it all.

Introduction

Imagine. Imagine there's no heaven, it's easy if you try . . . Do you remember the words to this deeply moving, well-loved song? The message of wonderful inspiration has grown even more potent in the 45 years since it was released by John Lennon. Why has it remained deeply loved all these years? Many of us get so touched that tears flow when we sing it together.

What do you imagine for your best life and the co-created life we all share? Is it possible we are imagining and creating our world, thus bringing it into being? Any creation starts first as a dream. Millions of us have a dream of a different world.

The Achuar people, an indigenous tribe in Ecuador free from outside influence until the 1990s, believe we dream our world into being. Elders traditionally awaken very early in the morning to sit in circle. As they share their dreams from the night, it provides direction for their day.

A group from the United States was drawn to Ecuador to help them protect their rainforest lands in the mid-nineties. This prompted the development of The Pachamama Alliance, a non-profit organization. The Achuar told them how much they appreciated help with the rainforest. However, their most vital work was in the United States to inspire their own people to dream a new world into being, as the current dream is now a nightmare affecting all life on earth.

That motivated the conception of *Awakening the Dreamer, Changing the Dream*, a powerful mind-expanding symposium offered around the world since 2006. Tens of thousands of people have attended—for so many of us want to dream a new dream. My passionate involvement for seven years as a facilitator of the symposium, and trainer of budding facilitators internationally, opened me to envision my own dream.

My dream came in a moment and my vision gets stronger all the time. I see people collaborating for the good of all; no debt or bills exist so all are free to create and share their greatest talents; nature, including all living things are respected and lovingly cared for; people are healthy, fit, and eat clean simple food; the pace is slower so everyone can relax and enjoy life; children are raised with love and elders have an ongoing role of importance; death is no longer feared but is understood to be a transition of the soul; communities work together to care for each other's needs, freely sharing all they have; the living is simple, creative, and satisfying. What is your dream?

The best working example of my dream is the Ubuntu project created by Michael Tellinger of South Africa. Ubuntu means, *we don't do anything unless everyone benefits*. Michael has been evolving his concept of creating sustainable communities for more than 15 years. He calls the sharing *Contributionism*. A small town of five to ten thousand people is ideal. It begins when residents receive free power in exchange for three hours contribution weekly to one of the community projects. This beautiful vision expands to free food, and eventually free everything as one small community takes care of each other. This working example called *One Small Town* is rapidly expanding worldwide.

Are you aware of the Workaway and WWOOF programs? They are part of the dream. I jumped into Workaway in 2013 when my volunteer application at a healing sanctuary in Mexico was accepted. As a newly single woman, I had only a small amount of money to live on but awesome skills as a healthy elder.

I was keen to experience living in a foreign country.

These exciting programs are available in every country around the world, connecting travelers with hosts who need help in exchange for room and board. A trade of approximately 25 hours a week gives hosts help with any project from creative people around the world. The energy exchange from different cultures, languages, and customs is an incredible sharing and uniting of goodness that creates so much more than just a little work exchange. One plus one is far more than two.

When I arrived at The Sanctuary, I became kitchen manager and stayed for four months. It completely changed my life. The sharing of healthy vegan meals, mind expanding workshops, sound events, and simple living with like-minded people who want to create a better world was amazing. This gave me a bird's eye view into the bigger changes occurring. Our planet is in good hands. The dream I have is held by people from all over the world. Thanks to social media, I have ongoing opportunities to see what my new Workaway friends are creating.

We can get lost in the system and feel isolated, desperate, and alone with the discord in the world around us. If we choose to accept mass media like TV and newspapers, we may be tempted to accept the status quo and give up. Sharing my dream is for those of us who innately know there is another way, even if we cannot see it clearly yet. Can you feel that knowing deep inside? Let's trust our greater vision and believe it is unfolding.

We can't see it clearly, but we are in the midst of creating this new way to live. It often looks like chaos because things must shake apart for change to come. We are pioneers similar to those who set off in ships or wagons hundreds of years ago with no idea what they would encounter and how they would survive. We are the pioneers of the 21st century. We need superb inner trust, support of like-minded people, and great stamina. Let's claim our knowing, hold our new worldview as a precious gift in our hearts, and share it with those open to seeing. We all need a supportive network to keep us strong.

I thought I was healthy, for I had more energy and zest for life than people around me. But what does health really mean? Just because I still had all my body parts, had never suffered a major illness, took no medications, had never worn glasses, and had abundant energy, I thought I was okay. I even became a Zumba instructor in the same class as my daughter and began offering local classes in my fifties.

Five years ago, I was having health challenges that I was just accepting. Honestly, I did not know it was possible to turn them around. The paradigm of expecting declining health is strong. My challenges included ten years of incontinence and digestive issues somewhat like irritable bowel symptoms. I was carrying at least 30 extra pounds of body weight with a lot of it held in a muffin-top above my waist. I was developing a dowager hump that kept me from being able to stand up straight. Yet my biggest stress was hanging onto a marriage that no longer held joy. The illusion of feeling healthy was actually based on being in better shape than most people I knew.

My journey on a holistic path cited in the chapters ahead includes reversing all the previously mentioned conditions. I am now living a vibrant life. My passion for health and openness to walk my talk has shifted me to new levels of vibrant living in all aspects of my life. Synchronistic events have taken my holistic expression of what is possible far beyond my imagination. It is exciting to feel so light, radiant, fit, and free.

When we see our lives holistically, lifestyle becomes fundamental. Lifestyle includes our thoughts and beliefs, how we nourish ourselves, the attitudes we immerse ourselves in, self-love, and self-care. Being a lifelong learner with a love for new experiences is vital. We all have choice. Knowing that at least 90 percent of all illness is caused by stress elevates the importance of relaxation exponentially. Freedom comes from taking simple steps to release ourselves from the deep emotional issues we all have. More steps to freedom unfold as we claim our inner power. It is not necessarily easy, but it can be done by making the choice and taking step by simple step. Incredible healing and vibrant energy can be the reward.

Though I have worked with food, movement, beliefs, and self-love, the biggest boon to my health has come from freeing my body of old unresolved emotions. I now have the most lean and fit body of my life. My memory is keen, clear, and even improving. I can walk, cycle, run, hike, travel, and whatever else I choose to do. My vibrant energy stays strong. Where is this going? What is even possible? It is so exciting to be alive, feeling confident and positive, with a passion to inspire others on this journey we all share.

Despite the trials, challenges, and growth pains currently being experienced in the midst of this Great Change, I see the result of our transformative work—we courageous pioneers. My dream continues to flourish as I hold my vision, inspiring me to offer love and encouragement to all I meet.

Knowing that the field of consciousness is energy we all share, I give my dream extra focus. I step forward with love and acceptance for all my decisions in life. Each one has brought me to the woman I am today. I accept my power and *response-ability* for my choices, beliefs, and all that I create from this point forward. I transform my fear.

I choose love.

Truth · Universal Love · Tenderness · Rebirth · Purity · Grace · Virtue · Transparency · Empathy · Quintessence · Truth · Beauty · Unity · Freedom

ONE

Choosing Our Beliefs

In medieval times, a citizen was arrested for having his own ideas and speaking freely about them. He was tied and taken under the baron's castle to the dungeon. Down dark stairs, down, down, he went, led by a ferocious looking jailer who carried a giant key a foot long. The door of a cell was opened and he was thrust into a dark hole. The door shut with a bang and there he was.

He lay in that dark dungeon for many, many years. It seemed like a lifetime. Each day the jailer would come, the great door would creak and groan open as a pitcher of water and a loaf of bread were set down before the door closed again.

One day the prisoner could take it no longer. Escape seemed impossible. Perhaps death was the only way to be released. He decided to attack the jailer the next morning as he was sliding the bread and water in. The jailer would likely kill him in self-defence and he would be freed from his misery. He went up to examine the cell door more closely to be ready for the morning. Going over, he caught the handle and turned it.

To his amazement, the door opened! Looking closely, he found that there was no lock upon it and never had been. For all those endless years, he had not been locked in, except in belief. At any time he could have opened the door if only he had known it or been curious enough to check. He assumed it was locked. The jailer's huge key was just an illusion. Leaving the cell, he groped along the corridor and found his way up the dark stairs. At the top, two soldiers were chatting but they ignored him. He crossed the great yard without attracting any attention. There was an armed guard on the drawbridge at the great gate. He as well paid no attention to the prisoner and he walked out a free man. He could have done this at any time through those long years in the dungeon if only he had known. He was a captive, not of stone and iron but of false perception and belief. He was not locked in, he only thought he was. Of course this is only a legend. Or is it?

It's an exciting time to be alive. To change any beliefs we first must be willing to examine them. Unexamined assumptions create the most havoc as they operate unseen. Embracing a vibrant life requires that we stop and examine assumptions or beliefs as we catch our thoughts. Hmm. Ask, is this really true? Can I absolutely know it is true? Be curious. Check the door. (like the prisoner) Let's move beyond outdated ideas when they are holding us back. Open yourself to a learner's mind like an innocent child and discover how little we really know. And what we think we know can change in an instant.

Even more powerful than the paradigm on aging in the Western mindset is the one surrounding health. Dramatic changes are available. I am now asking myself every morning: What is possible for me today? In what ways can I get even more vibrant?

My release from the prison of the paradigm on disease came early. Before I was a teenager, I observed my mom. She had surgery to remove varicose veins in both legs. I still shudder at the memory of her incredible cries of pain as she lay in bed and it was worse when she moved. My older brother helped her put on elastic stockings and get to the bathroom.

Years later, the surgeon's wife and Mom were at a social event in our small town. Somehow the topic came up as Mom noticed the woman's awful looking varicose veins on her legs. "Oh I would never have that surgery done," she exclaimed. That was a game changer for Mom to realize that even with a professional's opinion, we still have choice and the surgeon's wife refused the operation.

Years later when I was a teenager, Mom was scheduled to have her gallbladder removed. I went with her into a rather dark, dingy, strange-smelling store. It was the new health food store in our little town—owned by an elderly couple, Joe and Vi. Mom asked about options instead of surgery. Joe told her that he knew people who had successfully used alternatives. He photocopied some sheets of information about a lemon and olive oil drink. It is possible to release the stones lodged in one's gallbladder naturally. Mom followed the directions, had success, and cancelled the surgery.

Mom lived another 30 years and never had gallbladder issues again. It is for our own well-being to ask questions, get educated, and seek options. Fear and assumptions can make us agree to invasive treatments immediately. But the conditions we are dealing with are created over many years and it makes sense to seek options and education instead of rushing into something we may regret. There may be times when immediate action is needed, but often it's not.

The first step is to know we are prisoners of our deeply held beliefs, especially those engendered by the society we live in. Our own beliefs are hard to see—it's a bit like trying to see your own eyeball. They often show up as assumptions so it is valuable to ask, "Is this really true? Can I absolutely know it's true? Could there be another way?"

> *Beliefs have the power to create and the power to destroy. Human beings have the awesome ability to take any experience of their lives and create a meaning that dis-empowers them or one that can literally save their lives.*
>
> ~ Tony Robbins

It is incredible that our belief system is still based on Newtonian physics, which is hundreds of years old. Even Stanford University states that quantum physics has a completely different reality but we are not living it. Here are the main differences:

Newtonian

- *Everything is solid and we are separate from it all*
- *Consciousness is generated from the brain*
- *There is only one reality and it is linear*

Quantum

- *Everything is made of energy with no separation or empty space*
- *Consciousness is nonlocal which is profound as it is not inside our brains but is everywhere*
- *There is more than one reality and it is multidimensional*

Our bodies appear to be solid matter composed of molecules and atoms. This Newtonian thinking of solid masses and separation needs an update. Quantum physics tells us that every atom is more than 99.9999% empty space. Thus our bodies are bundles of vibrating energy that we direct with our thoughts, perceptions, and beliefs. The world we see is not true but we have been conditioned to accept it at face value and staunchly defend it.

Baby Boomers—people born between 1946 and 1964—are generally open to new possibilities for a healthy lifestyle. Additionally, there are many pre-Boomer bright lights in their 70s, 80s, and beyond that defy the aging paradigm. An amazing amount of focus is put on all manner of antiaging products and procedures. Many of us are doing all we can to stay healthy, active, and productive. It's inspiring to see. Yet as we really grasp that we are fields of energy, we will move beyond sickness, aging, scarcity, and poverty to radically affect change. It's unfolding for Boomers to be the generation to make this paradigm shift which is not just a small pocket of change but a total shift in consciousness.

We can move beyond old ideas about how the world works. It's time for change and new choices. Anyone can step on the path to vibrant living. How? Make a decision to be free and check the door (your assumptions), to discover new possibilities.

Scientists in the field have known since the late 1990s that our reality is our own creation. But this vital information has been withheld from the Western world. We live in a morphogenic field that responds to us with what we deeply believe is true. Shamans, wizards, witches, and medicine people have been aware of this, and some call it magic. So yes, magic is real. We are so much more powerful than we were taught.

All forms of media are still stuck, advising that health is determined by our genes. It is generally accepted that genes control all or most aspects of our lives. The nucleus in each of our 60 to 75 trillion cells was thought to be the command center. Dr. Bruce Lipton discovered this is a mistake in biology. He found it was an assumption made years ago that was never proven but simply accepted. It is now known to be false as his research clearly shows. However, this belief lives on in millions of people's daily actions since it is perpetuated across all media including scientific research journals.

I recently heard a shoe saleswoman advising a customer about inserts and surgery for foot problems. She said that her customers with a genetic predisposition to really bad feet, based on family history, had less successful surgeries. Just notice how deeply this belief about genes is ingrained. I hear it all around me. How about you?

Dr. Lipton discovered the genes we inherit that run through our families are only 10 percent or less responsible for illness. What about the rampant belief that we cannot escape these family patterns? If we believe that the genes from our families dominate our lives then there is nothing we can do. This leaves us as powerless victims where we give up and accept the inevitable.

But our genes do not control biology. It is our *beliefs* that affect our genes and our behavior. We are *not* powerless victims of heredity and fate. This is empowering and can help us make positive new choices. It is a brilliant use of our time to explore this truth by watching Dr. Lipton's talks on YouTube or by reading his book titled *The Biology of Belief*. He has gone the extra mile to get his wonderful message out to the world.

Let this empowering and life changing information sink in. Our beliefs create our predisposition to illness and aging. Beliefs outweigh our genes by at least 90 percent. Why don't we know this? As Dr. Lipton states, "It takes at least 10 to 15 years for science to take a proven fact from its first inception and release it to the public. But since knowledge is power, lack of knowledge is lack of power." His discoveries about beliefs and genetics, brought forward in the 1980s, were ignored. As a professor teaching young medical students outdated and incorrect information, he terminated his university position.

His ongoing mission and passionate intention is to bring the truth to the general public. Despite the invincible paradigm controlling science and health, he has been doing his best to educate and empower us. Dr. Lipton wants people to know they are not victims of heredity. Though his research was not accepted by science at the time, it has now been given recognition with a new designation called Epigenetics, which means above genetics.

This branch of genetics is devoted to the study of how and why environmental signals can mutate gene expression within the body. This is already changing the way mainstream science thinks about evolution. It is through Epigenetics that we can see the true power of human attitude and its electromagnetic effect on our DNA.

~ Richard Rudd, *Gene Keys*

Recently, a famous movie star chose a double mastectomy as prevention for family genetics that seemingly predisposed her to breast cancer. This shows the incredible power of our beliefs. Her story is a dramatic example of extreme decisions we can make when gripped by fear of death and illness, cancer being one of the biggest.

My older sister Lois discovered a lump in her breast when she was only 31. On visiting her physician, she was told it was probably nothing significant as she was young, not to worry about it and follow up with a return visit in three months.

In three months, the lump had increased in size and she was also experiencing pressure in her armpit, making her fingers tingle. Since she was a registered nurse, she was aware of the complexity and complications of lymph node involvement. Her doctor now wanted to do a biopsy to confirm the diagnosis, but my sister refused. If the biopsy proved to be malignant the next step was a mastectomy.

Being a true pioneer, my sister believed that if we give our bodies what they need, they will heal. She used medicines of the earth, the many natural healing herbs available for us. Sometimes she made them into a tea to drink and other times into a poultice placed on the tumors in her breast and armpit. Fasting, drinking healthy juices, and eating natural foods were important aspects of her healing.

Once when I was visiting, we drove to an organic farm and bought a fifty-pound burlap sack of beautiful freshly dug carrots, some with a little soil still on them. We took them to her home to make juice. Carrot juice is loaded with goodness and she drank lots every day. Vitamin and mineral supplementation was also part of her journey. Our eldest brother was deeply involved with the health industry, owning several stores in the Vancouver area and serving as President of the Canadian Health Food Association for three years. He greatly supported her on her healing journey.

My sister studied extensively to understand the process of cleansing, regaining, and maintaining her health. She was guided by a natural healer who helped in many ways and introduced her to the potential of using frequencies of energy to bring her body back into balance.

She had a complete recovery. The impact on her life and our whole family was huge. She left her career as a nurse and began to study in the field of holistic health where the entire person is considered rather than only treating the part that is diseased or injured. Her studies took her into energy healing, starting with Therapeutic Touch and Healing Touch. She taught these healing modalities to those in the nursing profession and anyone interested in learning the ways of healing with energy.

Once the door was opened for me, I was drawn to find my own answers about health and confirm my own truth. It began in my teens, continued intensely through my 20s, and became a life-long passion. A lot of it was really just common sense.

Through my 20s and 30s, I thought my friends would share my excitement to learn. I felt privileged to look at other points of view. I took nothing at face value, continually looking deeper. Most of my friends were not able to join me for my ideas went against the grain, sometimes in a big way. I relied very much on my birth family for support, though they all lived far away.

I had access to extensive information about fluoride's toxicity and the fact that it was banned in many countries. When I shared this, it was too radical. Fluoride was in all the toothpaste, and the dental association advocated topical fluoride for everyone along with a cleaning. I worked for four years as a dental assistant and quietly disagreed. But years later when it showed up as a weekly fluoride rinse in our tiny local school, my children did not participate. It is not easy to stand up for what we believe when it goes against the flow, but we get stronger when we trust our own wisdom.

When my research showed me the truth about vaccinations, it was like heresy. My first baby was soon to be born and I began to plan a way to avoid having him vaccinated. My mother-in-law cried. She said it was an awful thing to do to an innocent baby, to deprive him of the vaccines that would keep him safe from the ravages of horrible diseases. She truly believed that the government and the medical system exist to protect and take care of us. We simply did not agree.

Our first son had two or three vaccinations, our daughter one or two and I was finally strong enough to say "no" for our third child. My husband agreed with me but it was not his nature to take a stand on such a controversial subject against his own family. Our eldest son was ten and our daughter seven when our third child was born. During those years, two life-changing events happened, which strengthened my resolve.

The first was my uncle, a healthy man in his 80s, who was pressured to have the flu shot and finally agreed. He had no health problems before the shot but his reaction put him in the hospital and he died not long after.

The second was my nephew who was a toddler. He was vaccinated with the regular shot, which included whooping cough. He got a serious case of whooping cough shortly after. My mother helped to care for him and was scared to see how sick he was with the horrible sounding cough and the length of his recovery.

Our community health nurse, Betty, also a local farmer's wife, was curious about us saying no to vaccinations. She said, "I have never seen any information against vaccines. I can see you are an intelligent woman and you must have good reasons. Do you have any information to share with me?" I lent her my classic favorite, called *Every Woman's Book* by Dr. Paavo Airola. It covered all women's issues including menstrual cycles, pregnancy, and children's early years. I knew Betty had to do her job as a health nurse and provide services people wanted. Her work helped support her family during challenging farming years. She never questioned me again after reading the book.

My common sense said to keep our bodies strong and boost our immune systems with healthy *real* food rather than ingest small amounts of disease via a vaccination. I did my best to offer homemade meals from our big garden and also supplemented with vitamins. We were a vegetarian household from 1977 onward. There were very few trips to the doctor or the hospital and yet we were grateful to have that option when fractures and other accidents occurred. We avoided medications and let illness run its course. I truly believe that our bodies know how to heal if we can help them to do so. It usually requires a detox, like a good house or car cleaning, and simple clean food. It was not easy to have such different eating habits, especially for our children, but maybe it made them stronger too.

Essentially, if we change our beliefs, we change our genes. Let's move beyond this fear that aging and sickness go together. We are not susceptible to the diseases of our parents or our extended families. Whether or not arthritis, dementia, Alzheimer's, cancer, or diabetes has been present in our families, we have the power to change it. We are not predisposed to any condition. We can reclaim the choice to be healthy.

Remember that the genes we were born with respond more than 90 percent to our beliefs and less than 10 percent to the body we inherited from our family's gene pool. Let's really take that vital information in. Our beliefs, lifestyle, healthy choices, and determination to deal with old emotional issues have a much larger impact on our health and well-being than our genes.

It is a process to consider our beliefs and understand that our world is malleable. We are making it up every moment, according to what we perceive, believe, and thus expect. It takes contemplation but it's really not that hard to understand. Whatever we have in our lives is the result of our beliefs, and they can be changed when we have the courage to examine our ideas and assumptions and make new choices. If we don't make a change, we end up where we are headed.

Years ago, close friends and family members worked with The 3 Cs of Life, which came on a little card. We hung it in our kitchen as a reminder: You must make a Choice to take a Chance or your life will never Change.

Seeing those words was a potent reminder. They were also a source of much merriment and belly laughs as we saw how entrenched our desire to stay the same can be. Let's choose to take a chance. Let's choose what we want to believe rather than be stuck in an old prison cell. Consider the possibilities for humanity with such incredible open potential.

We can make the choice to look at life in a fresh, new way, refusing to allow previously held attitudes to have the power. I see how many people have that intention and openness. Let's intend that a whole new life can unfold for us, commit to it, and open to support others and be supported. Our committed intention has great power. We are all unique, powerful humans. Let's focus on developing our intuition and reclaiming our inner wisdom. When we have an open, curious mind, we can make decisions based on our common sense.

We have all lost some of our power by trusting too much in the professionals or experts instead of ourselves. Many of us see that experts in health, science, farming, finances, religion, government, and other areas are not dealing with issues in the best way. And, thankfully, many of us are willing to step up and speak out when we see the truth.

We offer inspiration and courage to each other by our actions. Perhaps this is all we need. We are all needed to step into our light and brilliance and share our passion with our world.

Gregg Braden, author of *The Spontaneous Healing of Beliefs: Shattering the Paradigm of False Limits*, talks about a power that lives within each of us. We are born with the ability to heal our own bodies, bring peace to our families, communities, and between nations. The power of our beliefs literally rearranges the molecules of our world to create our relationships, abundance, healing, peace, success, and more, all linked through the inner power of belief.

There is nothing noble about shrinking. There's nothing selfless about dimming your light. And there is no competition if the game you are playing is to be fully yourself.

TWO

Choosing How We Age

People don't grow old.
When they stop growing, they become old.

~ Anonymous

During the 1990s, I became obsessed with the wisdom put forth by both Louise Hay and Deepak Chopra. I loved listening to Deepak's message with his melodic voice and accent. In fact, I completely wore the cassettes out. One favorite inspirational story was about a tribe of runners. The young were fit and ran fast, those in their 40s ran even faster, but the fastest runners were in their 70s. That made such a deep impression on me. I simply believed that it was possible, for it resonated as truth.

But as I approached my 50th year, I began to dread the unknown change of life called menopause. Women around me shared their horror stories. It was uncomfortable to hear my friends and other women discuss the pitfalls that lay ahead. Many of them visited their doctors and were prescribed drugs for hot flashes and other symptoms. Some had their uterus removed and agreed to other surgical procedures.

I had been cautious about medical intervention after watching my mom and others around me. During my first pregnancy, I read a book called *Mal(e) Practice*. It detailed how women, as opposed to men, bought into having something wrong with them that needed fixing. I contemplated women in other areas of the world without access to drugs and surgeries. How did they cope?

I asked my older sister how our mother handled menopause. My sister said Mom took a few herbs common for women in Asian countries and did well. So my sister declared, "I want that too" and she breezed through it. I decided that if they could both choose easy, I would too; and I did. Apart from hot flashes, which were not that intense, I simply had a slowing down and then stopping of my menstrual cycle. I did not realize how powerful a declaration of choice could be.

Huge industries exist to medicate and operate on women. The majority of a woman's body is considered better when sprayed, douched, deodorized, colored, drugged, and surgically treated. Some doctors even said, "Once you are past child bearing age, you do not need your uterus. Let's just remove it and things should be fine." When we yield to Western medical practices, complications can befall us later when parts of our bodies have been removed. You go forward with your body, not the doctor, so trust yourself.

The senseless pressure on women to be fashionable with high heel shoes, and a wardrobe that needs constant updating feels wrong. But it is also hard to feel frumpy, out of style, and stop using hair dye. There is pressure from every area, including the media and advertising. We aren't encouraged to be our own radiant and unique selves.

Also, when women are in a cycle of competition, they can exert intense pressure toward each other. I was able to make peace with the fact that I was a woman in a world that seemed to cater to men who are deemed to get sexier with age. The image of a krone as an aging female in the Western world is scary and was never that appealing to me. I looked for an image that engendered respect and reverence for women too.

Losing our beauty, youth, strength, mental acuity, and ability to care for ourselves, contributes to the current epidemic of sickness in seniors. Yet, we are here at this cusp to make a change in this outdated paradigm. All of us are needed to make the shift by connecting with the awareness that we have choice. No matter where we are in the cycle of life, we can always choose again. This is not about seeking to live to 120 or beyond. It's about choosing vibrant health and freedom as many years as we live.

It's time to stop giving our power away to outside authorities—otherwise known as the experts or specialists. Listening to our inner guidance is essential to reclaim our power and make decisions that feel right for our own sacred body, and many of us are doing just that. It can be hard to have different ideas that don't fit in. Let's have the courage to trust ourselves, and support others to do the same. We all benefit when we stand up and share who we really are.

Making a Decision

In my late 50s, I had sessions with a well-known healer and author in his 80s. He radiated such wonderful zest, humor, and love of life. His wife was years younger than me. They wrote books and hosted workshops internationally as well as local meditations and private healing sessions.

His words resonated deeply as truth. "We each make a decision (usually unconsciously) about how we will age. It is based on how we see others aging in our families and society and also our beliefs. I can see you have not bought in to the status quo. You have chosen to embrace youthfulness." It was true. I refused to believe that I would need glasses, become decrepit or have a debilitating illness. Many are loyal to their beliefs about sickness and aging. We all choose.

In any society, people consent at a deep level to what is true. One term for this is consensual reality. Yet people live in different ways all over the world, see aging uniquely, and treat their elders differently too. There is incredible liberation in realizing we can change our world—including our health and our bodies—simply by changing our perception and taking action. Perception is a learned phenomenon that can be changed. All around me I hear others who are ready and open to make the shift.

Elders in Russia

People in specific areas of the world are famous for their longevity. In his wonderful book titled, *Healthy at 100*, John Robbins speaks about four separate groups that have been extensively studied. They inhabit remote areas in Pakistan, Russia, Ecuador, and Japan.

Abkhasia, located in southern Russia near the eastern shores of the Black Sea, is known as the longevity capital of the world. Studies showed an extraordinary percentage of people lived to well over 100 years, while retaining their full health and vigor. Some even claimed to be 150. Their remarkable health, vitality, and physical stamina were such that many of the younger researchers who came to study them could not keep up. They had sharp minds, high spirits, a relentless sense of humor and joyfulness, and they lived attuned to the rhythms of life. What can we learn from this?

The terrain is steep where they live and no one commutes to work and sits at a desk. Retirement is an unknown concept. They work regularly, at their own pace, in orchards and gardens. They often walk long distances of up to 20 miles as part of their day. They are remarkably relaxed, joking and singing as they work.

Of great importance is the tremendous respect for the aged. They are considered an indispensable, honored, and much needed part of society. Only the very oldest have wrinkles and white hair, more than a third of those over ninety do not need glasses, and most have their own teeth. There is no phrase in their vocabulary for *old people.* Those over one hundred are called *long-living people.* People gather for a yearly holiday and pay homage to the elders who dress in elaborate costumes while they parade before the villagers. Everyone grows more unique as they age.

One of the many factors to consider is their simple diet. They also avoid overeating. Children are raised with joyfulness. They all dance, sing, and celebrate life, unlike our Western world. They have a word for great, great, great grandparents. There is considerable importance placed on longevity, and the culture is very motivated to live up to it.

Even though we have very different cultures, there are simple and valuable steps we can take that will make a huge difference. First, let's make the choice to value and respect ourselves, whatever age we are. Together, let's create a new image of aging, opening a door to freedom and agelessness.

What thoughts could be holding you back from seeing yourself as a valued part of society?

> *Not long ago I unconsciously equated aging with the loss of mental agility, sensory acuity, physical limberness, sexual desire and a host of other human abilities. I thought it almost certain that we will all become more frail and disease prone as we get older. I thought that the best we could do was to be satisfied to accept these 'inevitable' losses with dignity. But the more I have learned from the people of Abkhasia, the more hopeful I have become. They seem to suggest that there may be another possibility for us entirely.*
>
> ~ John Robbins, *Healthy at 100*

In our youth-obsessed Western world, seniors are often thought of as a burden and are hidden away in retirement homes until they die. A senior with illness can be a huge burden of time, money, and emotions. We are taught to value younger people and devalue older ones. We all lose when we buy into these destructive beliefs for we will all mature and age. It is horrifying to see many seniors being discarded and left feeling useless and hopeless. So what can we do?

According to Deepak Chopra, we can rewrite the program of aging that currently exists in our cells. We turn into the interpretation of our beliefs. Let's use this awareness to create the bodies we want and encourage those around us to see that incredible possibilities exist.

> *Longevity is an individual achievement. It comes to those whose expectations are high enough to expect it. Our body holds great potential for improvement, even at very advanced ages.*
>
> ~ Deepak Chopra, *Ageless Body, Timeless Mind*

Let's face our fears and look at our beliefs. Awareness is always the first step. It's helpful to examine choices we have made. Taking time to write down your thoughts can be revealing. Where are you now? What are your fears? How do you choose to age? What keeps you from embracing life as an Elder? Take some time to honestly consider your current beliefs.

I choose the word Elder instead of senior. To me, the word senior is just another word for old, ready for retirement and the discard pile. Elder on the other hand is used to describe someone who has gathered wisdom and deserves respect. And this is how to proceed as we create the shift.

Paradigm Shift

Baby Boomers can be the ones to shift the paradigm by choosing a new way; we are powerful. There are approximately 76 million Boomers in the United States of a total population of 323 million, and 6 million in Canada with a total population of 36 million. It is possible to create a whole new picture of evolution as we claim a new way of living without the stigma of old age.

This new day will open up a paradigm shift of huge magnitude. But what does a paradigm shift really mean? It is defined as a fundamental change in an individual's or a society's view of how the world works.

How can we see our lives as a precious gift? How can we step forward as a respected Elder, instead of a discarded senior?

What do you see? There are at least two ways to see each photo below. Let your eyes play back and forth with the images you see.

Do you see an old hag or a youthful woman? Do you see a rabbit or a duck? Both can be seen in the same picture. Spend a few moments letting your perception play back and forth. This simply reminds us that different possibilities in perception are right under our noses. These photos are not new but are valuable reminders.

Paradigms are internal habits that have been embedded in our unconscious for a long time, especially societal ones. To think outside these societal norms or the status quo takes awareness and then choice. Remember the tribe of runners whose beliefs created greater strength and fitness as they aged? What is really possible?

Plant a New Choice

We can all choose a new thought. As we do, it is like a little seed dropped into soil. We have to pay attention to it, water it, and nurture it, which helps it grow and take hold in our life. Otherwise the weeds, established plants or old ways of thinking will overtake the new seedling. Our mindful intention to our new thought helps it flourish and eventually win.

Let's choose a new awareness and shift this outdated paradigm on aging. We cannot look outside ourselves for someone else to do it. We are the ones we have been waiting for. Let's trust ourselves and these exciting times. By feeling deeply into our own truth and acting on that, we are creating a new world.

We become Elders when we decide to stand tall and embrace this gracious term. No one bestows it upon us. Becoming an Elder means many things, including:

- *Choosing how we will live*

- *Choosing our energy, vitality, and health*
- *Choosing how we will die*

Do we have choice or control over such things? It is time to believe that we do. It's an illusion that aging happens in any certain way. It does not. Let's feel into the choices we have made with the information received thus far in our lives. No matter what they are, we always have the capacity to choose again. There is incredible liberation in realizing we can change our world, including our health and our bodies, simply by changing our perceptions, making new choices, and taking action. Yes, we can. Forget nursing homes and extended care as a destination. It may happen, but don't plan it into your future. It may come but it's not a given.

Choosing to See

Deep inside we know we have an emerging value. There is a place within us all that connects to this truth. The years as an Elder are a precious time of redeveloping our talents. We can open to a sense of joy simply at being alive in the time of Great Change for as many years as we are graced to be here. We can feel into the truth and find our self-respect and value. When we honor ourselves, our world responds in beautiful new ways.

Self-Love

The love we feel and shower upon ourselves is returned many fold. By loving ourselves, it creates more love in the world, and we take the burden off others to fill that role. No matter what kind of childhood we had, we can choose to parent ourselves with kindness and softness. Let's love ourselves, our uniqueness, and the gift of being alive. When we do, our inner radiance shines forth. One who glows with inner love and gratitude for life is a bright light wherever they go.

We can inspire each other to transform the paradigm on aging. Choosing joy, gratitude, and grace will open our Elder years to glorious new possibilities that we cannot even fathom today. We are living, breathing creators of a whole new reality.

Retirement

Let's release that old, made-up concept. It only creates fear and lack of worth or purpose. It is a natural evolution to change the work we do throughout our lives as needs, desires, and different opportunities arise. Our life experience is needed on the planet now. We are all being called into action, but in a different way than going off to a job. Our job as Elders is inside first, to realize our own value and honor who we are. This is our time to take a slower journey inside. This balance is needed now in our Western world of instant gratification and speed.

The following chapters offer inspiration to engender self-respect and value, not only as an Elder. We all deserve respect and value, regardless of age. Self-love and self-forgiveness are potent healing modalities. We will cover them more extensively. So take heart if you do not yet feel in a place of honoring yourself. It will come. We can all learn new ways to see our value.

One tool is examining our beliefs about aging. Contemplating our fears about losing our abilities, getting sick, and being unable to care for ourselves can be safely transformed. The simple act of writing down our fears, concerns, or any other feelings onto a page is healing. As Junie Swadron teaches in her lovely book *Write Where You Are*, the simple process of writing out what is true for us gives healing and release. It can be easy and happen quickly.

It is essential to find ways to forgive. Forgiving others is mostly to free ourselves, for we carry the burden inside us. When we work with the pain and challenges of life, they turn into our wisdom. Otherwise, that unresolved pain could become the excess weight carried on our bodies, or the pain that shows up as illness.

Pain always comes to help us, not hurt us. The message pain brings is a gift when we inquire deeply and pay attention to what it is telling us.

Passion and Pizzazz

Is it possible that our passions and skills can come together to fill a need in the world? We are each a dot that makes up the mandala of life on our planet. Each of us is needed. As our passion and pizzazz are stimulated with respect, support, and cooperation, our roles as cultural creatives for the new world will unfold. We can trust ourselves at this most auspicious time to be alive.

Remember that we each declare ourselves an Elder when ready. Most of us missed all the celebratory rites of passage through the different stages of life. We claim our own designation as an Elder and a new vision for our lives from this time forward. We are each unique. As we feel into this truth, let's find new ways to support each other in stepping forward with our true gifts for the good of all. We can create the support we need. If you are 30, 40 or 50, create your own ceremony as a rite of passage to honor your life.

Living into my 66th year, I fully opened to embrace my life as an Elder. I saw my value in expanded ways. I realized that a part of me was avoiding the Elder chapter of life. The door opened, allowing me to see endless possibilities, including being happier with my body and my life than ever before.

I am strong, lean, and fit with a great memory, wacky humor, and zest for life. I want to share my greatest gifts for as many years as I am graced to be alive. To love and accept myself, just as I am, while encouraging and inspiring others to do the same for themselves, is a worthy endeavor. It is so possible to live with energy, vitality, full mental capacity, wit, laughter, and joy. As I open even more to possibilities, I see magic and miracles all around.

Right of Passage as an Elder

I was waiting for years for someone to set up a *Rite of Passage* ceremony for those of us entering the Elder chapter of life. Finally, I realized it is up to me. This ancient way of celebrating our passage through the different stages of life can be reclaimed. We can bring it back. I hope to inspire a surge of Elders claiming their best life ever.

Create your own ceremony, when you are ready, in your own unique way. Invite a few close family members and friends or the whole town. Speak of your life in whatever capacity feels like your truth. Claim and embrace respect as you move into life as an Elder. State your clear intentions and joy as you claim this chapter of your life. Claim the juiciest and most enticing version you can imagine. Declaring your intention out loud, in front of others, is powerful. Let it be witnessed by at least one person who loves and supports you. Since you are unique, choose what feels right. You are a powerful Elder, creating what you want, not a young child waiting for someone to have a party for you.

Choosing How We Age

With every experience, you alone are painting your own canvas, thought by thought, choice by choice.

~ Oprah Winfrey

As an Elder, there are many areas of life to speak about, so choose your own adventure. Embracing the gift of being a *long living person* is amazing. It creates a shift, and expands your confidence, courage, and joyfulness. We can choose to take the time and space to explore juicy places inside. Share what feels right as it enriches you and inspires your guests who listen with love. More complete details are in Chapter 7.

Let's stand tall, create this for ourselves, and encourage others. It is a new day when we choose to support and encourage others in our community. By stepping into the Elder chapter of our lives with joy and enthusiasm, we are shifting the paradigm on aging. It is a great gift to have life experience and community support as we do.

The essence of who we each embody is meant to be alive at this most challenging and amazing time to offer the vast and infinite wealth within us all. Our unique radiance, as we claim it, helps those who are younger to learn and grow into their highest potential. We can choose to bring a different perspective with wisdom, ideas, and time to those who need it most in our world.

Let's demonstrate the possibilities of an incredible life as part of our contribution to the whole. Dessert really is the sweetest. Taste it well. It is quite the magical gift.

THREE

Choosing Our Attitudes

The greatest discovery of all time is that a person can change his future by merely changing his attitude.

~ Oprah Winfrey

Were you taught to choose your attitude? Sounds silly now but I thought it just happened. As a teen, I was quite a rebel with a bad attitude. I seemed to fall easily into smoking, drinking, and partying. Even as an eight-year-old, I got my friends in the neighborhood and my younger sibling smoking. It seemed grown-up and cool. My poor mother. I did not know that the stew of emotions and attitudes I was brewing was a choice, and that it hurt others as well as me.

As a young wife in my late teens, and as a mother a few years later, I seemed caught in a swirl of acting and reacting to a life I just did not fit into. I knew I was acting out with anger, inflicting my moods on others, and basically creating my own hell. My husband once told me I should have been a Philadelphia lawyer as I could talk him under the table. The power of attitude and how it shapes our lives seems obvious and simple now, but it wasn't back then.

Understanding my choice with attitude came slowly over the years. I began to realize how thoughts, feelings, words, and actions go together. One philosophy I studied had a popular saying: Thoughts are Things. That meant thoughts had extra power, but were they within my control? Around 17,000 thoughts come and go in our minds every day. Can we decide what to do with each one, moment by moment? Is it possible to simply observe our thoughts without being attached to them?

A huge turning point came for me when my eldest child was a teenager. One day he came in the house with a lippy attitude to get out of mowing the lawn, with a ride-on mower no less. It triggered my old rebellious nature and there I was outside tackling him, punching him, and then holding him down, pinning his arms to the ground. It shook me to the core, and him too, to see how enraged I could become in a flash. A friend delivering fuel in our farmyard saw what happened. It was scary to know my rage was so huge, that it was beyond stopping or hiding.

As the rage slowly subsided, I realized I had become just like my father—something I had sworn I wouldn't do. It was time for change. I joined a group called Adult Children of Alcoholics at the recommendation of a friend. That caused a big stir in my birth family and with my husband. Why would you admit to that? Was your father really an alcoholic? I learned about different perspectives, family secrets, and the pressure to conform.

It did not matter. The secret was out. It was my first attempt to say my life is not working, and I need to change. The anger and rage inside me were huge and terrifying. Sometimes I felt my rage would explode if I were to take the metaphorical cover off to deal with my issues.

The Adult Children meetings were great to learn about family patterns. Over the months, those attending continued to vent the same old stories of victimhood and pain with little apparent movement forward. After going through all twelve steps, I realized I had been stuck long enough. My strong intention was to get through it and become a better, more peaceful person. I wanted to heal. I knew the submerged rage was not healthy for me, and indeed was dreadful for those around me when it emerged.

Then my sister Lois sent me a book by Louise Hay called *You Can Heal Your Life*. It came at the perfect time. It was a pretty white book with a colorful rainbow on the cover. Reading it triggered my anger so deeply. Louise wrote that we all choose to come here and that we create whatever is in our lives. Wow. I just wanted to fling the book across the room. It was hard to accept that if I was not happy with my life, it was up to me to make some changes. It felt easier to blame my husband, my remote farming location, and my busy life with three children. But as long as I stayed stuck blaming others, I remained the victim unable to claim my power. It was pretty scary to take full responsibility for my choices, yet it's the only way to move forward into freedom.

> *To transcend the state of a victim depends on our attitude. It's not about what happens to you. It is about how you handle it.*
>
> ~ Richard Rudd, *Gene Keys*

I began to consider my dreams and desires. What did I really want from life? They were pushed down pretty deep. I had been taught through example in my family and culture that women take care of the house, the yard, the meals, and everyone's needs. My needs, dreams, and desires? I did not have a clue what they were. I just knew I was not happy. But first I had to deal with the anger.

Affirmations courtesy of Louise Hay, my ongoing heroine, were my next project. It was hard to find a private place to speak the words. "I love myself, I love myself, I love myself." I felt so silly. My family got quite a kick out of it and made fun of Louise's angelic voice on her cassettes. It truly made me wonder if I was crazy to proceed. But the memory of the overpowering rage toward my son kept me going.

I was blessed to attend personal growth workshops called "The Psychology of Vision" with Chuck Spezzano, thrived as a member of Toastmasters, and developed some better listening skills. Then I found NLP (Neuro Linguistic Programming) through a book my younger brother Bryan suggested, called *Unlimited Power* by Tony Robbins. I devoured it and was captivated, becoming a practitioner at trainings in Vancouver, a master practitioner, and eventually a trainer on the Big Island of Hawaii. It was a time of great processing and change in my life.

It was clear I needed to leave my marriage. I still had hopes for a miracle, but I knew the pain and disconnect we created together was numbing and drying up the juice inside me. I endeavored to leave with the least hurt possible.

From the outside, our lovely white home, three healthy and smart children, and my husband and I as a nice couple looked good. But inside the walls, communication was sparse and tense. It seemed painfully empty and filled mostly with the sound of the TV. Alcohol and overeating were used to numb the pain and cope with life.

We did seek a counselor to find a way to stay together. But it was an awful experience as he was used to helping clients with much more serious situations. We left his office feeling ashamed that we could not get it together and find a way to be happy.

NLP turned out to be my route to healing painful emotions, for which I will always be grateful, and it eventually became a business working with clients and offering workshops. Through it I learned that no matter how huge my anger or anyone else's emotions are, it would not blow up my office. And no matter what anyone looked like when they walked in, we all have the same feelings inside.

It was a relief to feel more peaceful, yet difficult to split the family apart. The pain of that is huge, but trying to live the lie is worse. A message from deep inside said, "Couples think they can stay together for the kids, but that just models how to endure an unhealthy relationship."

Self-Love

I continue learning more about love. Although volumes have been written on the topic, most of it is about yearning for love or pouring out our love toward another. Self-love? Isn't that kind of selfish? Who loves themselves first?

Thank goodness for Louise Hay and her deep understanding that we can only be healthy when we take care of ourselves first, and then our life can flow.

> *Love is the great miracle cure. Loving ourselves works miracles in our lives.*
>
> ~ Louise L. Hay

I now begin my day with gratitude for my bed when I first awaken, and to my body for the gift of another day. As I open my eyes I say, *I'm alive. I have one more day. Good morning bed, thank you for being so comfortable and for such a great sleep. I love you. Dearest Cori, this is a blessed day. All is well. There are great experiences coming our way today and there is time for everything we need to do.* Could this gratitude be the reason I usually sleep well anywhere?

Then I rise, use the toilet and look in the mirror, right into my own eyes. I choose to resist any temptation to be critical of messy hair or anything else I see and I greet myself warmly, speaking these words with a smile:

Dearest Cori, I love you, I really, really love you.
Thank you all sixty trillion cells of my dear body for keeping me healthy and strong.
There are terrific experiences coming our way today.
You look wonderful, you have the best smile.
Your skin is lovely and firm, your hair is beautiful and unique.
You are my ideal woman.
The Universe is For Me.
I love my life, I love this day, and life loves me.
All of life is organizing in song around my success and I am very grateful.

I have these words on a little card taped to my mirror. This is my reminder, which helped me memorize the words. Affirmations are not new but they have become my consistent daily practice over the last year. It sometimes feels silly, but silly is better than too serious. Now I do not care what anyone thinks for I have seen the difference. It is one of my priorities as these words of encouragement and self-acceptance set up my day powerfully. It takes time but what an incredible use of the first few minutes of the day to add vibrant energy. If you choose to do this mirror work, find words that feel right for you.

My friend Bev shared an analogy that we each have a barrel of apples. Self-love and self-care fill our barrel. Each thing we do that makes us feel good adds an apple. Each thing we do not want to do—but do anyway—takes an apple. If we say yes when we want to say no, it takes an apple. If we put someone else first instead of lovingly taking care of our own needs, it takes an apple. If we do not choose enough nourishing events each day, by learning to say yes to ourselves, we soon end up with an empty barrel.

Many of us grew up in the era of putting more importance on doing for others than doing for ourselves. Symptoms of an empty barrel can make us feel cranky, tired, and sometimes ill. When we feel that way, it's important to notice how we are caring for ourselves. We must choose to love ourselves and honor our own needs, because no one else can do it.

There is nothing more important than learning to love ourselves. I am always learning more and deepening what I know. How amazing to learn that when I love myself, my life flows. I am the one who will always be there for me. I deserve love simply because I exist.

I also like to repeat Deepak Chopra's words from *Ageless Body, Timeless Mind*. "I am perfect as I am. Every experience in my life is working toward my ultimate good. I am loved and I am love."

Strong inner direction that it was time to write brought me back to the snow globe in Canada from the beautiful summery warmth of Central America in January. But I could not get writing and found the best excuses in the world to avoid it. Then a synchronistic moment brought Junie into my life when I saw her poster on a bulletin board at a ferry terminal. Within a few weeks, I had hired her to help me. As my new mentor with more than twenty years as a writing coach, she was able to see that my self-judgment and lack of deep self-love were stopping me. Using the program from her book *Write Where You Are*, I was able to do some deep writing to those I felt most judged by. Then I discovered they were only reflecting my deep self-judgment. Letters were written to release my feelings onto the page. They are never sent or seen by anyone. That makes it safe to let it all out.

As I uncovered layers of self-judgment, I found a deep desire to be adored. I recognized that I secretly wanted adoration in my relationships. It feels funny to admit this, but it stems from a deep need of the younger me. When I imagine her big eyes looking into mine, I can shower her with the adoration she wants. It satisfies a deep need. Reaching back to embrace the younger me has opened my heart and helped me support myself more fully.

Writing this book, to share my deepest ideas, practices, and thoughts has brought up shadows like deep criticism, self-judgment, and fear. I am grateful to have simple and effective ways to process these shadow parts of me. More extensive processes for transforming old emotions and attitudes are in Chapter 4, Choosing Freedom.

> *Because of the heightened sensitivity of your DNA, everything in your life from the food you eat, to the people you live with, is co-creating your body via your attitude. Your attitude determines the nature of the electromagnetic signals that reach your DNA. For example, if you are having a bad day and find yourself in a negative frame of mind, this attitude will generate a low frequency impulse throughout your body. Your DNA will respond to this by shutting down certain hormonal pathways in your brain and you will feel sad, depressed or frustrated. On the other hand, if you are having a bad day and are able to break out of your negative mindset and laugh at yourself, a high frequency electrical signal will reach your DNA and you will feel lighter and more joyful. Your DNA will respond by activating certain hormonal signals that will lead to your day feeling much brighter."*
>
> ~ Richard Rudd, *Gene Keys*

Laughter

Can we choose laughter as an attitude? To laugh at oneself and the foibles of life is a great gift to all. I have always loved to laugh along with my entire birth family. When we would gather and tell stories, the huge belly laughs would sometimes continue until the tears flowed. It was fun and therapeutic. Two of my three brothers could have been stand up comedians. The hilarious way they could interpret ordinary situations was priceless as we discussed our years growing up. The mimicking, voice-overs, and funny ways they could twist a situation would have us all in stitches.

Once at my brother Bryan Pepper's home, in the middle of the night, we were talking and laughing our heads off. My sister-in-law came out and said, "What? You crazy Peppers. Laughing and talking all night!!" Few people in my life are so much in love with deep belly laughs as my family.

Although our lives were far from perfect, our parents were honest, hard working people who raised seven children well. I am grateful to have learned so many basic skills—like cooking and sewing. A good bowl of homemade soup is still a family specialty. My mother kept a clean, orderly home and baked bread and cinnamon buns weekly. What a treat to come home on Wednesdays to bite into the still-warm bread with melting butter.

My father was a farmer. His whole family came from Saskatchewan in the dirty thirties when lack of rain drove them west. He understood the value of nourishing the soil. Every spring we put manure on the garden patch. Phew. Some years it was a little ripe and the smell wafted through the whole neighborhood. We grew sacks and sacks of potatoes and other veggies. Dad built a cold room to store root vegetables, and we preserved the rest in various ways.

Dad loved to fix and tinker with anything from clocks to cars. He said, "If some guy can figure out how to make this, I can figure out how to fix it." He often had extra parts once the fixing was done, which made us all laugh. He hunted and fished to help relieve the incredible pressure of nine mouths to feed. He taught us all to drive a standard vehicle, change a tire, check the oil, and many other basic skills. There were challenges for sure, like his explosive anger, but the journey through life is to learn and grow and I later found out that my parents did a better job than many.

Two years ago, a few of us got caught up in a complaining match about the state of the world. Thankfully, our friend Cody Bear shared a story from Harry Potter when the students are being taught to cast a spell. They are told that whatever thoughts or fears are in their mind will show up in their creation. So if a monster shows up, it was part of the fear in their mind. But how could they deal with a monster? If they turned to run, it grew bigger. They were taught to yell, "Ridiculous!!" When they yelled "Ridiculous" out loud, the monster got smaller. "Ridiculous!!" It shrinks again. In essence, our life is all made up and has no power unless we believe it's real. We choose. When we say "Ridiculous!!" it is easy to laugh. It helps us remember it's all our creation. Sharing this Harry Potter story with more friends and family has opened up a network of people who enjoy this "Ridiculous" understanding, have a belly laugh together, and take life less seriously.

Later that summer, I was helping at my sister and brother-in-law's vegan café. It was a particularly stressful day. My sister Janice and I were working alone and it got so busy that we had no break until supper time. Since I was new to procedures and the menu, it added to the intense chaos just to get through the day.

I woke up in the night having a panic attack. This was a brand new experience; I was unable to breathe and my chest was tight and painful. My heart was beating like I was running a marathon. Whew. This panic attack was connected to the anxiety from the café. I settled myself using my tuning forks to shift the energy and help me rest. I was not used to the pace in a busy café, which brought out my serious side. I forgot about being "Ridiculous."

What a great reminder. During our morning walk along the beach, I related the Harry Potter story to Janice, and how calling out "Ridiculous" causes the threatening energy, which seems real, to disperse. We reviewed our lives and busy times at the café, all the while calling out "Ridiculous" as various events were brought up. We both began laughing uproariously. It completely changed our relationship and our work together. The fun of it continued and we never let any situation have the upper hand. We have a new, light-hearted relationship. Stress at the café fell away, just by having that "Ridiculous" understanding.

Life can be so funny—depending on how you see it—because life always throws us curves. It does not matter what happens, it's how you handle it that matters. You can always stop, be aware of what you are creating, and choose again. It is your life, so how do you want to live? Sharing this with your circle of friends creates more laughter and fun. A week, a month or a year from now, the issues you are stressing about will not even matter; move beyond them now.

Did you get chastised for too much giggling like I did as a child? I also felt compelled to stop my children when it seemed like their laughter was getting out of control. Why do we frown on too much laughter? Research from a blog called Ageing Healthily, Happily and Youthfully says the average four-year-old laughs 300 times a day, but an average adult laughs only 13 times a day.

Just observing children, it is obvious they laugh much more than adults. Why? We can all benefit from laughing often and long, so let's choose it.

Norman Cousins, author of *Anatomy of an Illness*, had great success using laughter to heal. He discovered you can double your heart rate while laughing. Cousins reported that ten minutes of belly laughing reduced his pain for two hours and he needed less medication. Laughter lowers cortisol, a stress hormone that can weaken our immune system. In one study, watching funny movies for 60 minutes significantly increased the level of interferon-gamma, a hormone that fights viruses and regulates cell growth. Norman Cousins was a great pioneer, using laugher and Vitamin C to recover from an unusual onset of paralysis when he was hospitalized and not expected to live.

My dad married Betty when he was 88 and she was 92. A widow for forty years, Betty joked that she had been looking for a *younger* man. My sister asked a reasonable question: Why get married at this stage of life? Dad said that Betty was not the kind of woman to shack up. She wanted a commitment and a ring on her finger. Our whole family attended their sweet wedding.

Betty was a jokester and a natural comedian. She and Dad met when the woman at the desk noticed his violin as he moved into a seniors' residence. She commented, "If you play that thing you need to meet Betty and maybe you can entertain us with some music. She plays the keyboard." Their love of music, dancing, and sports drew them together and soon they were a couple. They played old-time music from the thirties and forties. The laughter was good for them. Betty had been a dancer all her life, and Dad as well, so they would put on some music and dance in the evening after dinner. How lovely. They moved from the seniors' residence into a townhouse and seemed happy in their short time together. None of us know how long we have, so each day is precious.

Betty moved to an apartment after Dad died. She led chair- and walking-fitness classes there in her mid 90s, and got up with her line-dancing group to entertain us at her 95th birthday party. She was an excellent example of the tremendous power of laughter and fun. Not expected to live as a baby, she fooled everyone living a full 98 years. She had no obsession with good food, but created her health with an active joyful life, the openness to try new things, and the choice to see humor in daily events.

She and I joked about Christmas being so overdone, and we agreed that it was too much all at once. One year she crocheted red, white, and green hot mats and sent them as a gift in July. We had a good laugh about that. She really looked for ways to make an ordinary day fun.

She who laughs, lasts.

~ Anonymous

Have you heard of Laughter Yoga, created by Dr. Madan Kataria, from India? Laughter yoga is growing in more than 70 locations around the world—without advertising—because of the benefit people are receiving. Our inner landscape does not know whether laughter is real or fake. Laughter changes our mood in moments by releasing feel-good endorphins. It strengthens our immune system and works against the negative effects of stress—the number one killer, and depression—the number one sickness. When your body has enough oxygen, you feel more energetic. And when you have enough laughter, it helps you stay positive.

I tried laughter yoga hesitantly in Mexico. I had heard of it but never liked the idea of a fake laugh. In the beginning it does feel forced or fake; but before long, the laughter is real and natural. It is described like starting a cold engine. We have to coax it along until it gets warmed up and rolling.

It was surprisingly easy to laugh and our group felt so much lighter and joyful at the end of the class. For days after, meeting each other in the house caused spontaneous belly laughs. No reason was necessary. I have a warm spot in my heart for every member of that laughter yoga group. Even years later we break into wonderful, hilarious laughter just seeing each other. We can choose our attitude and find endless ways to laugh.

Joy

Belly laughing brings the flow of spontaneous joy flooding into my body. Joy comes from my body's response to life, not from an event. Choosing to feel joy is what creates joy. Then observing anything around me can magnify it. Witnessing the miracle of life in a child, the sky, a tree, a flower, or a beautiful meal can create the flow of joy inside. When joy wells up inside me, its incredible energy connects me wherever I am and I feel so grateful to be alive.

Gratitude

Gratitude is another choice in life. When I choose to be grateful, I feel my heart open. Life really is a miracle. Our bodies are a miracle. We each decide how we want to see and experience life. Gratitude cannot be taught. It does not come when we receive something. It comes when we choose to be grateful for what we already have. Then whatever happens, our lives are infused with richness. To be grateful for what we already have, as often as possible each day and before sleep, makes life flow.

I consider self-love, laughter, joy, and gratitude to be the essential building blocks of a healthy, vibrant life. And we each get to choose how we infuse our lives with their goodness each day. As well as choosing to see life from these powerful perspectives, another part of transforming is to shift our old behaviors and beliefs with our presence and acceptance of them, just as they are.

It's so exciting to accept ourselves the way we are and not wait for some imagined perfection. Let's have compassion and simple kindness for ourselves and this human journey we are on. When we are as gentle with ourselves as we would be with our dearest friend, our lives rapidly shift for the better.

FOUR

Choosing Freedom

No one saves us but ourselves. No one can and no one may. We ourselves must walk the path.

~ Gautama Buddha

Dealing with unresolved emotions is a big key to health. I have believed, lived, and worked with this truth for twenty-five years. It has been extensively tested in my family life as well as with clients and friends. Yes, food, exercise, and other aspects of a holistic life matter too, but they get more attention. Our unresolved emotions, also called our shadows, have more impact than previously recognized, but they continue to be avoided by many. It can feel harder to deal with emotions and see their connection to our health and well-being. As Louise Hay said, "The issues are in the tissues."

On the home stretch to finishing this manuscript, Spirit gave me an opportunity to check what I truly believe. Talk is cheap. Walking it is not as easy and is truly all that matters. I am forever grateful for these lessons.

I was inspired to contact Balboa Press to explore self-publishing this book through them. I got a call back from a lovely, interesting, and engaging woman. We had a great connection and I could tell she was really listening to me. She made me a wonderful offer to publish not only this book, but to re-publish my first book, called *Vision Quest, A Spiritual Awakening.* I took Vision Quest as far as I could on my own, 10 years ago. The offer from Balboa included some generous discounts.

Connecting with a subsidiary of Hay House was huge for me. The options offered to authors in the publishing programs seemed so comprehensive. I was in the midst of hiring an editor but Balboa seemed to have it all. I was made an offer I could not refuse. I knew from my first self-publishing experience that it is hard to learn and do it alone. But when I said yes to Balboa and made a plan for payments, life events slowed me down. First I got some advice to be really clear about the offer and what I was paying for.

The messages began days before that. After an enjoyable 30-kilometer cycle along a tree-lined trail on beautiful Vancouver Island, I stopped for a delectable Indian meal. Emerging from the restaurant, I discovered my rear tire was completely flat. Thank goodness it happened after I got back to town! But it was so flat I could not push it and had to lock it up and get help from a neighbor with a truck to bring it home. That was the universe trying to slow me down but I could not see it yet.

A few days later, I made my decision to go with Balboa. I woke up normally and within an hour, I got severe lower back pain and suddenly could hardly walk. It is such a common tendency to think, "What have I done to strain myself? Did I pull a muscle?" But being a Louise Hay fan for nearly thirty years, I knew that lower back issues were connected with fear about money and not feeling supported by life. I had committed to pay a lot of money from my budget and I was stepping way out of my comfort zone.

My back told me so when I asked for the message, which is an important first step in healing. Pain is always a messenger when we can open our ears and our hearts to hear. The pain was so severe that I could hardly get up and down. I had to take the day away from my computer and my writing. Then I had to take the next day off too.

I know from my research with back pain that it can be the result of a dehydrated body, and I have seen quick recoveries from hydrating with water. I drank lots but it did not help. Then I did some stretching exercises, which did little. Suddenly the severity of the pain opened my eyes. I had no adverse effects from my long cycle a few days before as I am quite fit. Then in a moment I was bent over, hardly able to walk, feeling pain with every move. It was humbling. I suddenly realized the significance of my flat tire. I do not own a car and the back tire on a bike is the power driving us forward. I was also unable to get it fixed for several days which was another big clue to slow me down.

Our bodies are so brilliant and we can also find the answers all around us. If we look with an open mind, we find them. *You Can Heal Your Life* provides that insight and also a new thought pattern to work with to help shift outdated thinking. The one for a painful lower back is, "I trust the process of life. All I need is always taken care of. I am safe."

Then I used a technique called Vaporize the Victim to find and transform the old emotions connected to back pain, like fear of not having enough money and feeling unsupported. I spoke with the fear, to make sure I was getting the message from the pain.

Fear was worried as I was moving too fast. When I asked for a symbol of the fear, I saw myself as a young girl, just shaking with fright. Using Vaporizing the Victim, I was able to simply be present with the younger me. I am safe to be seen now. I have a plan, I have help and the details are handled so it will all be okay. But the younger me did not know that and the job of fear was to protect me, which is a valuable thing. Fear is our ally and needs to be understood and thanked for doing its job and then it can be worked through.

I continued with Vaporize the Victim identifying other patterns, such as fear of being seen. I had a flashback from twenty years ago. I walked into a spiritual bookstore in Edmonton, Alberta. A big beautiful display of Louise Hay's books, tapes, cards, and other offerings was right inside the door. As I looked around with admiration, the scene shifted and I saw *my face* on all the items displayed. It scared me back into my little cave. I was terrified of being seen. Using Vaporize the Victim, I asked the memory of that old emotion to show me a face and worked with what came up.

I wrote a letter to my back. Using directions from *Write Where You Are* requires no theme, writing experience, good grammar, or spelling skills. The requirement is paper, a pen, and the willingness to just write. I also wrote to other people in my life as I felt guided. These are sometimes angry blaming letters. They are NEVER meant to be sent. They are meant to be an external landing place. All I know is that it works. It always amazes me how quickly my life shifts and I have stopped trying to figure it out. I usually burn the letters as I hold nothing back and would not want them to be found by the wrong person. Find a safe place to write and let the truth of the moment flow onto the page. It is healing, revealing, and it cleanses and releases in a simple way. I love using this process. It is so much better out of me and safely onto a page. You might be surprised what comes out once you get rolling.

I spent time lying on a light blanket on the grass in the backyard, under a down quilt, *earthing*. This simple and powerful way to connect with the energy of our earth brought balance and healing to my body in a tangible way.

In the evening, I remembered how healing gratitude is. I like to sing things out which is more powerful than speaking, and a lot more fun too. There are endless things in life to be thankful for. Though I had a sore back, the rest of my life was awesome. Saying a heartfelt thank you makes a difference right away. Then I found a little ditty. The words are: Oh the Lord is good to me, and so I thank the Lord, for giving me the things I need, the sun and the moon and the apple trees, the Lord is good to me. This was brought to my life by a great book called *Thank You Power* by Deborah Norville. I immediately felt better when I sang that fun song. It also made me laugh at myself, which is always good.

Within one day, I was healing well. The pain was nearly gone. I was taking it slowly and mindfully. I found a new, more comfortable place to sit and write, and I also made the choice to stand at the kitchen counter in front of my computer. With new ways to support myself and be more relaxed as I write, I show respect and care for my body. As my friend Nola says, standing is better as a lot of sitting just gets us in trouble. She's right.

My steps were: taking ownership of the pain and asking for the message; seeking guidance from *You Can Heal Your Life* with the new thought pattern; working with all emotional patterns to transform them with the steps in Vaporize the Victim; writing letters to fear and pain; and employing heartfelt gratitude with songs and words.

It's time to create freedom in every way, and this chapter holds the keys with my favorite processes. We can learn to easily move from an emotional victim state to one of power. This accelerates our own evolution and that of the whole. Some processes are my favorites from 20 years ago, and some are much newer. They are all very effective. By the way, in just a few days, I was 98 percent back to normal. A little tenderness on one side remained, to remind me that a breakneck speed is not useful. Once I really slowed down to listen, that tenderness disappeared too.

You Can Heal Your Life—Asking for the Message from the Pain

I have owned this book since my sister gave me my first copy in 1988, cycling through copy after copy as I passed it on. My kids never liked it when I brought it out. But as adults, they all have and use their own copy, and sometimes they are the ones to remind me. Over the years I have worked with many clients, using the book to ensure I have covered all aspects of their issues. It is like being a detective and never ceases to amaze me how perfectly the condition fits the mental patterns and how it all flows together.

In the early 1990s, I had my first experience of finding an emotional link. I woke up with a very sore throat and felt exhausted. After getting the kids off to school, I collapsed back in bed. My husband said, "Oh you must have that flu that's going around." No way, I thought. I got out Louise. A sore throat is holding back something you need to say. I asked my inner wisdom what I needed to say. The message was to cancel the Mandarin study group meeting at our home. If the message feels like, "Oh no. Anything but that," you have found it. I plucked up all my courage and called Myrna. "Oh, I was wondering when you were going to tell me, she said. I can see how busy you are." Sheesh. After that I drank lots of water, rested for the remainder of the day and was 100 percent the following morning.

The Being Process

Everything we see is a reflection. Reflections show us, in others, our beautiful qualities we enjoy. Reflections also show us hidden, disowned beliefs, behaviors, or patterns in others that can be hard to see in ourselves. There are useful ways to work with and interpret these reflections that will come clearly upon your contemplation and willingness to see. I first was shown a way to transform the stuck energy of our emotions in 1995. It plopped into my head as a vision.

I called it the Being Process, for it is about the willingness to simply BE with whatever emotion or pattern has shown up. Although it was simple and efficient, it seemed too simple and the concept difficult to accept. When I guided clients and others through the process, they had success but had trouble when working the process on their own because they could not understand how it could be so simple. It easily brings old patterns into balance inside, which shifts our outer world.

Have you ever felt blindsided by a distasteful situation in your life? You were just going merrily along, minding your own business, when out of the blue—whack. How could it have anything to do with you? It must be the other guy and his stuff. Following are two samples of how the Being Process works. I share them as inspiration to show we can transform outdated or stuck energy patterns. Eckhart Tolle, Arnold Patent, Panache Desai, Debbie Ford and other leading-edge thinkers have similar steps to easily shift old emotional patterns using the power of the present. The most challenging part is finding your own unique process as we all do the work somewhat differently.

The Bully and The Victim: Tanner's Story

Grade six was really cool. I was proud to be in the highest grade. The kids were friendly and it was great to see them all again since I spent summer away on the farm with my dad. I was especially glad to see the twins, Darryl and Darren. We all enjoyed playing lots of basketball.

Near the end of September, a new kid named Joe joined our class. What a geek. We didn't like each other right from the start. Soon he was bugging me and pushing me around on the playground. He was tricky and did so when the teacher was looking the other way. I told him what I thought of him, which just made it worse and he bugged me every day after that.

When I told Mom, she started asking me questions like, "What do you see in this kid?" She said he was just acting out some old parts of me. I really hated it when she said that stuff. He was such a geek. I did not want it to be true. How could I be anything like him? She tried to get me to do her process with the things about Joe I was seeing, but I refused.

It got worse and worse until one day in November. Joe got a bunch of kids together after school and followed me to the twins' house. They lived near the school and we went there to play basketball. Joe was such a creep. He kept giving me shots to the head and saying come on, fight. No way. I wasn't stupid. Then the twins' mom came home and broke it up. Boy was I relieved!

I went right home and told Mom. "Okay that's it," she said. "I was letting you handle it in your own way, but now it's gone too far. If you get hurt, it affects both our lives so let's get this sorted out." I didn't want to, but my mom refused to take no for an answer.

Mom made a list as we talked. First she asked me about the things I saw in Joe (1 and 2). Then, we talked about the way it made me feel (3 through 7).

1. *Attitude—dumb*
2. *Doing stupid things without thinking like smoking*
3. *Revenge*
4. *Hurt*
5. *Anger*
6. *Unfair*
7. *Fear*

Then Mom asked me to bring all seven qualities one by one into the power of the present, which brings a balance. "No way," I said. I knew how to do her process because I had used it before but why should I? "Joe is the one coming after me," I said. "It's not fair that I should do the work and he gets off scot-free."

Mom explained that all we can ever do is take care of our own stuff. We can never change anyone else. She said, "When you release these stuck emotions, you will shift the energy and the seven things on your list will cease to have a connection to Joe." I could see that the first two things on the list might also apply to me. And it was not the first time I felt the five emotions on the list. But I stubbornly refused. Finally Mom resorted to bribery and agreed to rent me the Nintendo game I wanted for the weekend if I did the work. I agreed.

When I do the work, it is really easy—it's just not

my favorite thing to do. First I imagine I am floating up above my head, and I see all the colors that flow like energy through the spot where my body is. When I think of a word on the list, it has a certain color; anger is usually red. The red flows in with every other color swirling where my body is. When the red and all the other colors are flowing evenly, I know it's done. Then I move down the list, and the next word takes on another color. It took me less than ten minutes to complete.

Soon we were off to the rental store. I did feel a whole lot better. The next day our principal called Joe and me down to the office. Someone had reported the fight after school. We got a lecture on the terrible example we were setting for the younger kids. He called it a gang fight and warned us that no more fighting would be tolerated. He made Joe and me shake hands.

Joe never did pick a fight with me again. He still got in trouble bullying other kids on the playground, but he never bothered me again. It was funny because I kind of liked him. By the end of the year we were getting along quite well.

If you examine any negative trait you insist is present in another person, you will find the same trait is hiding in yourself. The more you deny the trait, the more strongly you will have to project it.

~ *The Path to Love*, Deepak Chopra

Mr. Patient: Dave's Pattern

When we start to observe ourselves, there can be surprising discoveries. A willingness to own the reflections in our mirrors is powerful. We may see many unexpected patterns. It often brings up repressed emotions that are quite unfamiliar.

I met Dave while hosting a three-day workshop related to observing and understanding our thought patterns, how they create our reality, and how to shift them. Dave was a quiet and likeable guy who spoke softly and said little. Being a retreat, everyone stayed overnight. But Saturday evening was an important family occasion so Dave went home to attend.

I noticed him returning early Sunday morning, and we went for a walk to talk. He was upset and said the party was not that good. "I got so angry I wanted to hit someone. What could be happening to me?" he asked. "I am always patient. In fact, I am well known for my patience."

"How has that served you over the years to be so patient?" I asked.

Dave hesitated. "Not always so well."

"Have there been times you had to hold back what you really wanted in order to live up to being Mr. Patient?"

"Yes, I have held back a lot," he sighed.

Dave had sacrificed a lot of his true nature in order to live up to the role of having so much patience. He was shocked at his strong reaction. I assured him it was very natural when we begin to reclaim our wholeness or all aspects of our nature. There really is nothing to fear. Dave had taken the role of the patient one. Patience or impatience is neither good nor bad. They are both necessary to come to a place of balance in our lives. By using the process, Dave was able to be more real with his feelings and own them. Many of his stronger emotions were simply covered up with the role of being Mr. Patient.

Dave's process was seeing the event that caused him such irritation in his mind's eye like a movie. As he sat and breathed, staying present with the discomfort, it dissipated. It can be quick to process when we stay present and gently focused. Breathing with awareness helps. Then the test is simply to think of the event, and when the charge is gone or it feels complete, it is!

Wholeness means all qualities: the patience and the impatience, the anger and the calm, the love and the hate. Wholeness is all of them combined which flows and creates a balance. This allows us to respond in the moment to situations in our lives from a balanced center, which opens our truth now, instead of living by rules or conditioning of the past.

There has been a tendency to want to release, let go of, or get rid of certain behavior patterns. Where do they go? There are no spaces in the flow of the universe. Could the paradox be true? Could this stuck energy transform when allowed, accepted, and embraced?

It only seems like a paradox, but it is powerful to realize we embody all of the qualities that exist. The ones we do not like become our shadows. We may or may not want to acknowledge them all, but they are there. It does take courage and honesty. The more foreign it seems to you, the more deeply the pattern or shadow is hidden within you. Living life from these shadow patterns can keep us in a victim state and our world in chaos.

What I called the Being Process back in 1995 is found in a simpler version called Vaporizing the Victim from *Gene Keys* by Richard Rudd. This brilliant book changed my life in a very short time. Vaporizing the Victim offers simple, clear steps to freedom.

Energy can neither be created nor destroyed; rather, it transforms from one form to another.

~ Einstein

The Shadow and Vaporizing the Victim

This wonderful way to transform our shadows, or outdated emotional patterns, works in minutes. Remembering that energy changes form is vital. This simple process allows us to make rapid shifts in our lives and reclaim our power to move into freedom and choice. It suppresses nothing. Instead it honors whatever shows up and opens the energy flow to transmute it. When patterns like anger, pain, abandonment, fear, self-judgment, or any others show up, the power of our focused presence and breath opens the stuck energy. This allows the stuck energy to be free. It is simple and effective.

When we Vaporize the Victim, we fully embrace our shadows. We accept all of who we are. Our issues come from disowned emotional states. These parts we all have are called shadows. Depending how deeply we have disowned them, we see them acted out (in someone else), like I did when I thought others were judging me. Richard Rudd, author of *Gene Keys*, also created a webinar that gives more detail about the process. He describes how our consciousness on the planet is moving beyond the victim state to take full responsibility for ourselves, creating the gift of freedom.

1. Awareness is the first important step. When a shadow or unwanted emotional pattern has been triggered, remember that the shadow or emotional state is finite. It will pass. Realize this pattern has been triggered as an opportunity to heal it, own it, and honor it. The other person did not cause it. They triggered what is already deep inside.
2. Compassion for yourself is essential. Hold the belly, where our emotions mostly reside, and have compassion. Be gentle. Remember it will pass, so stay with the emotion. Breathe. That will keep you present. Be allowing, be accepting, and embrace whatever shows up. This pattern has been working a long time within your life. Breathe and stay present.
3. Transmutation happens in the belly. As you hold your belly with compassion, be soft. Give the shadow/emotion a face to allow you to connect. When you can, open your heart to it. Have fun with it. Stay present and breathe. Remember the shadow is finite. It will pass. Stay with it, and check your progress by thinking of the situation that triggered the shadow to emerge. That lets you check how things are shifting, and notice how the process is going. Allow, accept, and embrace the shadow in whatever face or symbol it has shown itself. Stay kind and gentle to yourself, and simply stay present with your heart open. This

> simple process rapidly shifts lives. It can move us from a victim state to a powerful place of healing and choice. Stay with it as long as it takes for the energy to change form. As you keep your focus with this simple process it gets easier and easier, like learning any new skill.

The main challenge, when guiding newcomers with Vaporize the Victim, is their tendency to make it complicated. Also, we do not recognize how powerful we are. For more information see genekeys.com or find Vaporize the Victim as a webinar on YouTube.

It's so exciting to accept ourselves just the way we are and not wait for some imagined perfection. Let's have compassion and simple kindness for ourselves and this human journey we are on. When we treat ourselves as gently as our dearest friend, our lives rapidly shift for the better.

With my awareness, I no longer take on the emotions that I feel. They are part of the field of consciousness and the world wound. I simply identify them and vaporize them to free the energy as a service to humanity and myself. I choose freedom.

We all have the option to enter this place where we stop identifying with the emotional states. Feel them and know they are real, but you do not have to take them on. Learn to no longer associate with an emotion such as anger by thinking, O*h this old anger. It's back again. When will I ever be done with it?* Don't take it on as a part of you, but instead vaporize it to allow the energy to flow freely to create something new.

Write Where You Are

With this wonderful book written by Junie Swadron, we are guided to simply write. If we are in pain, write to the pain; in sorrow, write to the sorrow; in numbness, write to the numbness. Write wherever you are without trying to get somewhere else.

When you are willing to just sit down and write, magic happens. Junie is my writing coach. When we first started working together, I became blocked. She guided me to see who I feared would criticize me. That fear of criticism stopped me cold, and I was unable to write.

I recognized that the people criticizing and judging me were reflections of my own self-judgment and self-criticism. Junie advised me to write the angry blaming letter, holding nothing back. I must admit when I read through that part of her book I felt above the need for that sort of letter. That is for other people, I thought, but it was perfect for me and it created miracles at the time and many more since then.

Once again these are not letters to ever be sent. It is just a safe and easy way to get the feelings out of you. Then wait a few days, and let there be a dialogue. Let the person respond back to you on the page, just letting your imagination tell you how they might reply. And then respond to that only in writing on the page. Yes, it's imaginary but potently accurate.

The details of these and other processes are in both of Junie's books, available in paperback and e-book. This simple, free-writing process shifted my life in days. The first person I wrote to phoned me unexpectedly and since then a clean, more loving, and respectful relationship is emerging. It is a miracle. I have suggested it to many friends who agreed that it shifted their lives too, when they had the courage to "just do it."

In a recent documentary movie created for Lifestyle Medicine, it is suggested that a focus on nutrition, exercise, and emotions can improve our health. But if we could pick only one, working with our emotions is the most powerful choice.

When we blame society or others for what is happening in our lives, we remain a victim. Any one of the choices in this chapter will help to shift us out of powerlessness, which is what being a victim is. We have no power because we do not take responsibility for our own lives. We have been taught to put it into the hands of the church, the government, the doctors, and other experts.

No one can make us feel anything. Instead, they trigger what is deep inside us. When we choose to face our real emotions, we create inner alchemy. When we choose to get to the root of stressful, unresolved emotions, we transform them and our lives.

Be flexible. If you are happy with your results, perfect. If not, be open to another path and keep asking to be shown what would work better. Trust yourself. Choose to see the world around you as perfection. Unity is the first essential step to living a healthy life in mind, body, emotions, and spirit. Each person, animal, insect, bird, and fish is meant to be here. No one is an island. We all need each other, for we make up one synergistic whole.

It is vital to reclaim our power. Once I fully employed the ideas I share in this book, including a mostly vegan diet, my body slowly got forty pounds lighter, and I now radiate more health and energy than ever before. I hope you choose and claim your freedom in whatever ways are right for you and remember you can always choose again.

FIVE

Choosing Our Fuel

Life is either a daring adventure, or nothing at all.

~ Helen Keller

In 1997, two friends and I set off on a road trip to Mount Shasta, California. It was a long drive from Alberta, Canada but it was the first week of May, and we all felt ready to explore after a long winter. Neither of them could share the driving since they didn't have experience with standard transmissions. So driving my sporty blue car fell solely to me, which was fine because I love driving and road trips. We sang songs and enjoyed rich conversations as we rolled along. Virginia had been to Mount Shasta for every Wesak Festival and shared some of the mystical experiences she and others had. Mount Shasta is considered a vortex or a portal. Ascended masters and other beings are sometimes encountered in visions and dreams.

Hurtling along at highway speed in southern Oregon, we were chatting about the possibility of beings in spaceships around us. Time stood still. Suddenly, I was aware of my hands on the wheel, of the cement blockade dividing the highway right beside me, and the speed of my little car. A moment before I was not driving. But where did I go? I woke up behind the wheel with all my senses heightened. All three of us realized we had shared a mystical moment in some other place or dimension.

Arriving at the Wesak Festival, we checked into our rooms and took a short walk up the mountain, which is often hidden in hazy clouds. The air was cool and the mountain huge and ominous.

We registered for the event with more than a thousand other people. The master of ceremonies was a lovely blond woman from Australia. The person beside me leaned over and asked,

"Did you know she's a breatharian?" I sat dumbfounded. A what?

Pranic Nourishment

In that mind-expanding moment, I stared at Jasmuheen's perfectly proportioned body and heard her gentle elegant voice complete with her charming Australian accent. I had never even heard the word breatharian. She had written several books on the topic and later I was introduced to other breatharians at the event.

Could it be true? Jasmuheen looked so vital. To realize she received most of her nourishment or fuel from the energy all around us like the sun and the air was a revelation. It opened a door of possibility in my mind. I met her in person after the event. She claimed to drink only a little tea for the enjoyment of it at social events but had no need for food as fuel. I am not advocating this for I have not personally taken this path. But this possibility is first in the fuel chapter since this awareness helped me systematically cut my consumption of food while expanding my energy and sense of well-being.

There are couples who practice modified versions of pranic nourishment. Husband and wife Akahi Ricardo and Camila Castello believe humans can be sustained largely by the energy of the universe. They eat a piece of fruit and a little broth a few times a week, just for the enjoyment of it. Akahi has created programs to help people lessen their attachment to food as fuel. It is a fascinating journey to even consider it. If we cut our dependency and consumption by even a portion of what most Westerners currently eat every day, it would make a huge difference. I'm sharing this as food for thought.

Others I am aware of who have taken this path of eating a few times a month are Kirby De Lanerolle and his wife from Sri Lanka. Their interviews are easily available on YouTube.

Listening to Your Body

My friend Nola and I used to laugh about taking a pranic nourishment path. After cooking all day to create a big meal, we questioned our motives. The shopping, washing, chopping, cooking, cleanup, money, and time spent could be used in other ways. Perhaps one day I will rely on pranic nourishment, but right now I just eat simply. I drink liquids until noon, a green smoothie for lunch and later things like simple roasted veggies or homemade soup with a salad. I like to eat an early evening meal. But being flexible is essential as I travel a lot and rules do not work. Instead, I trust my body for direction and delight in having less attachment to food.

I do not advocate any particular way of eating. I know what works for my body and I also know that we each find our own way through the endless choices for nourishing ourselves. Meals are best enjoyed with heartfelt gratitude and celebration. This is more important than what is on the plate or in the glass. And really it starts in the kitchen before we eat.

Dr. Masaru Emoto, a brilliant Japanese researcher who wrote many books, discovered that even the best quality food can shift to a low vibration when created with a negative attitude. With his analysis, the vibration of food or "hado for immunity" was measured. A factory made hamburger was -4; homemade was +10; homemade with loving words +16; homemade with angry words -6. Contemplate those numbers for a moment.

The loving words were: looks delicious, smells good, and can't wait to eat together. The angry words were: frustrated, tired, and

I don't have time. How often have we all felt that? Reading his books helped me create meals with love and joy and sometimes when I am asked for a recipe I acknowledge that love is the secret ingredient. Accounts report that in some monasteries, only the most experienced monks are allowed in the kitchen for they understand how important attitude is.

We feast again is a confirmation my friend Nola and I laughingly acknowledge during our friendship of nearly two decades. She puts on dancing music as we create our magic in her kitchen with good simple ingredients. A feast to us does not mean a buffet of excess. A feast is a beautiful, fresh, lovingly prepared meal. We both worked with chefs and know how to put little accents on a meal to make it divine.

A spoken blessing sets the tone to honor the fact we are so fortunate to partake in such a bounty as many do not. Various nourishing food and drink including smoothies, fine tea, or a full meal are celebrated with words of great gratitude.

Food is a huge topic with a strong emotional charge. It is much more than fuel for our bodies. People eat in endlessly different ways around the world. Food is connected to pleasure, pain, and also reward. Some have too much food and some have too little. I encourage learning to listen to your own body and following its direction as much as you can.

Eat simple, real food of the cleanest, best quality available. Local is great. I love to pick my own or pull it from the ground. It is generally considered best to focus on veggies, fruits, nuts and seeds, and healthy fats; have meat, fish, and grains as more of a garnish instead of the main dish. We are all so different that we benefit from trusting what our bodies want. We need to take the pressure off. We may benefit more from eating non-organic food in a happy, positive environment than eating expensive organic food in a stressed mindset. Food is important, but a holistic approach looking at lifestyle matters more.

I was raised on meat, fish, potatoes, veggies, and fruit, as well as bread and milk in its many forms. Eating this way caused constipation all my life and I remember my mother giving me Ex-Lax to help me have a bowel movement. In my twenties, I was still struggling with constipation and digestive issues. I ate less and less meat and intuitively felt I should stop eating it all together. It was a huge decision that left me sitting on the fence. I was married with a three-year-old and a six-month-old baby. It was time to add different foods to my baby's diet. Was I going to start her with meat or not? It was time to choose.

Some of my family, including my parents, had already embraced a vegetarian path. Since my eldest brother was now headlong into the health industry, owning five health food stores in the Vancouver area, it was easy to consider other ways of living. Most of my family worked in the stores over the years. I was too far away, but the most dramatic thing for me was access to information. This expansive opening to new possibilities for healthy living became my lifelong passion.

Undecided about eating meat, we had a steak dinner. When our three-year-old son woke us up vomiting undigested chunks of meat, I got my answer. Our household became vegetarian. This meant no red meat, pork, or poultry. My digestion and my husband's digestion improved right away. It was easy for me to recreate our favorite recipes minus the meat. We did not eat much fish at home, but it was something for our stupefied friends to feed us when we were invited for dinner and to order in restaurants. In 1978, vegetarian choices were sparse compared to today.

At first I thought vegetarianism was the key to a successful life. It was like I had found religion. I wanted my friends to have the benefits too. Most of them respected my choice but it was not for them. I learned to back off and honor the choices each person makes. I am currently mostly vegan and love it, having the best, most fit and lean body of my life. But when my body says it needs something different, I am open and flexible to eating some fish, eggs, or even meat.

Two years ago traveling in Guatemala, I had acupuncture with a gifted therapist. He mentioned that my digestive fire was enhanced during the session and would benefit from eating some meat, kind of like a reset. I had not eaten chicken for at least 15 years, but my body was craving it in a way that could not be denied. Hesitantly, I went out for a lovely dinner with my friend Joanna and included a small portion of chicken. Would I gag, could I digest it, or would it throw my system off? There were no issues. It digested well and I have not wanted it since. I am learning to take the charge off food and just eat what I need.

When I feel like a bag of chips, a muffin or a chocolate croissant, this process works really well. Instead of immediately telling myself no, I visualize myself eating it and notice how my body feels. Usually at the end of imagining myself chewing it up and having it land in my stomach, I realize I don't really want it. And if my body says yes, then I decide.

A few years ago, I was in the Canadian Rockies in a small community where I hosted a cacao ceremony. The following morning I was traveling by bus to Vancouver. I went into a restaurant to see what options there might be for breakfast. I was drawn to a veggie omelet with hash browns and toast. How odd, for I had not eaten eggs or this kind of breakfast for quite a while. I found it delicious and ate the big portion with gusto, just trusting. Within an hour, an accident on the icy winter roads forced a closure of this major highway. A semitrailer slid sideways on the ice and took out a whole row of power poles. Our bus was delayed for hours while the road was cleared of debris. The meal sustained me well for the trip. I was grateful as the only other option was junk out of machines.

What we believe about our food is the most important factor. Our bodies take what we give them and create according to what we believe. *We are what we eat.* Our foods become our body. And what we believe about how the food will affect us is the direction our bodies take. So if you believe you need a certain amount of protein a day, then you do. But if there was a truth about protein that applied to us all, then I would certainly not be healthy, being vegetarian for more than 40 years.

> *You have about 60 trillion cells in your body, all with different roles and responsibilities. But most importantly, every single cell in your body is doing two essential things: It is listening and it is responding. Each cell is listening to your environment through its countless molecular antennae embedded in the cellular membrane.*
>
> ~ Richard Rudd, *Gene Keys*

When we let our bodies guide us, we can keep it simple. We can let ourselves be right and enjoy what we eat. Nothing is set in stone. How we eat today can and will change. We are each the creators of our own life. Tomorrow we can make another choice. Let's eat with joy and inspiration.

Real Food

One key is to eat real food. A potato and an apple are real food.

Real food, like a potato, has no ingredient list. But when we buy a box of instant mashed potatoes, or potato chips, it is now a packaged concoction that is no longer real, even though it may be tasty. The life force in the potato is lost in the factory where it was processed and packaged. It becomes a pretend food with low life force and lots of calories. To be vibrant, we must give our bodies food with life or pranic nourishment directly from source.

Real food is optimally what we grow ourselves, like the kale, cilantro, strawberries, and parsley I have in pots in the yard. Two or three strawberries are so revitalizing right from the plant. When we make the effort to grow a little food ourselves, we know for sure where it comes from. It can also be the sprouts we grow on our kitchen counter. Sometimes communities have garden plots available for rent. There are many ways we can choose to put the highest quality energy and vitality in what we consume.

Local growers and farmers' markets are a wonderful choice for live food. Community-supported agriculture (CSA), a program that links consumers with farmers, is becoming more available. It's wonderful to meet the people who grow your food, and give them your financial and emotional support and appreciation. Anyone who has farmed for a living knows it can be hard, with barely enough financial remuneration to keep afloat.

Organic is great if possible, but it is a long process to become certified organic which makes it more expensive. Local ethical growers who use compost and natural rather than chemical fertilizers and sprays are available. Choosing to support these local ethical growers can take some pressure off your wallet and that support keeps them in business.

Worry and stress about food does more harm than good. Obsessing about finding the perfect food takes away the pleasure and relaxation of simply enjoying our fuel. Since stress is known to be the cause of 90 percent of our illness, let's take it out of the equation on food.

When we are gentle with ourselves and just do the best we can each day, a wonderful relaxation flows into our lives. Each day and each meal is a new choice. We vote and make powerful changes with our dollars, so let's put them toward the things that matter in creating the new world.

Protein

Our Western world status quo says we need protein. Some schools of thought even advocate counting the number of grams of protein consumed daily, suggesting meat, fish, and beans as the highest sources. Food combining so amino acids are complete can be mind numbing. If all that were true, I would likely be dead, or for sure sick and weak, eating meat only a handful of times in the last 40 years. I have also never done food combining, or calorie counting—ever.

This is proof to me, for me, that what we each believe carries far more weight than any actual food. I know it's not necessary to eat meat as so many foods have all the nutrients we need. I get my protein from high quality greens like spinach and kale, and other fresh whole food choices. It's not the amount of protein a food contains; it's the amount that is usable by our bodies. Meat is high in protein, but how much can our bodies use? Meat also has a high waste content, so it takes a lot more of our precious body energy to digest it. It tends to move slowly through our digestive tract, often contributing to constipation.

When we consider that the Western world, especially North America, has the worst track record for disease on the planet, and the highest consumption of animal products and processed foods, we must re-evaluate what the status quo has been feeding us. With two thirds of Americans obese, we simply must choose again. And the best part is, we can. Every meal, every day is an opportunity to choose again.

My life and my body dramatically changed, in numerous ways with a 95 percent removal of wheat and dairy, and 80 percent removal of grain about five years ago, so it is worth considering.

Wheat

Since my early 20s, I have carried a ring of fat around my middle, even though I was not really overweight. The bulge would disappear if I did a detox or cleanse, but it would quickly return. I fully bought into the myth that whole grains are healthy and enjoyed creating all kinds of breads and other baked goods for my family. We ate lots of rice, rolled oats, rye, and other grains. As grain farmers through the seventies, eighties, and early nineties, I did not suspect my belly had anything to do with consuming wheat. For a time, my mother and I even had a ritual of freshly grinding our own wheat to make yummy bread and buns.

When my daughter Carrie reported that she and her husband quit eating bread, I was very surprised. They were both feeling better and reported weight loss. Their inspiration was a book called *Wheat Belly*, by Dr. William Davis. I was somewhat resistant, but she persistently asked me if I had read the book. I had no idea how it would impact my life.

Statistics and studies from the book had me reeling. The most outrageous one is right on the cover: *Two slices of whole grain bread can increase blood sugar more than two tablespoons of pure sugar.* What a shock. I thought I was well informed about health, but the scam about whole wheat and healthy grains was held in my psyche. What a great reminder to keep reviewing our deeply held beliefs.

I was especially captivated by Dr. Davis's understanding of wheat's addictive properties. They can cause a roller coaster ride of hunger, overeating, and fatigue. For years, I was puzzled how some meals did not satisfy me very long. I could not possibly be hungry, but a short time after a meal I would be back in the kitchen scouting for something more to eat.

In the book, Dr. Davis explains how wheat has been hybridized more than 10,000 times over the past 60 years. It's no longer the grain it was in the fifties, but it's a completely different substance. This franken-wheat becomes addictive and acts like an appetite stimulant making us want *more*. Of anything. When I made this connection, I decided to stop wheat immediately. It was difficult until I got it completely out of my system, which took a while. The withdrawal symptoms can be severe, but it's worth it.

I had so many of the symptoms Dr. Davis lists as being associated with eating wheat, including foggy brain, swollen fingers, painful joints, addictive overeating, digestive problems with bloating and gas, and of course that bulgy muffin top around my middle.

It has been a process over the past five years, but all the symptoms I was experiencing have disappeared or significantly improved. Muffin top is gone, digestion and bowels are excellent, keen clear brain with a wonderful memory and addictive eating rarely surfaces. My fingers tell me with a little pain, or some swelling in my gut, when I have eaten too much grain of any sort. That is enough to keep me on track to keep wheat out of my life, and only eat other grains sparingly. My body tells me, I listen, and that's what matters. I am happy with my sleek body, strength, and stamina.

One of the challenging parts is simply finding all the places wheat is hiding. It's cheap filler in many processed foods and is even considered a food by itself—pasta. To remove wheat from your diet, you must read labels. This has been my practice for years. However, it is a shock to find how many innocent looking processed foods contain wheat. It is not easy in a world where bread has been considered the staff of life, but it can be done.

Refusing fresh homemade bread can cause hard feelings. Yet I know that just one taste can take me down a spiral path for days and, as a wheat addict, I might not get back on track again. It might sound impossible, but it is similar to being a drug addict when one is extremely sensitive to wheat.

That extreme feeling of addiction has subsided over the years since I got wheat out of my system. I can have a small amount occasionally now, but it seems to create a little bulge in my middle right away, which seems to be connected to an inflamed digestive tract. When we put sugar and wheat together, as in Oreo cookies, they are said to be more addictive than cocaine.

Dairy

I was never much of a milk drinker, but almost everything tasted better with a little cheese. My whole life I had a sticky, choking mucous in my throat. I knew for years it was related to my consumption of cheese, cream in my coffee, and delicious whipped cream on desserts. What was a cup of coffee without cream?

When I finally came face-to-face with my addiction to dairy, I felt ready to change. This is a showstopper in the Western world. Cheese is everywhere. It means saying no thank you to most of what is commonly consumed when dairy and wheat are taken out of the equation. I was told I had taken all the fun out of eating. But I did not care, for I was feeling better and better and, to my relief, the mucous in my throat disappeared.

The statistics about dairy are listed in *The China Study*, a life-changing book by T. Colin Campbell. This book states that the nutrients we seek from animal-based foods are better provided by plants. That includes protein, fiber, vitamins, and minerals; plants have it, along with major health benefits.

Over and over, studies show that people consuming the most animal-based foods have the most chronic diseases. People who ate the most plant-based foods were the healthiest. Whether vegan or not, they suggest putting as many plants on your plate as possible at every meal.

Milk is food for a baby goat or calf. We are not meant to steal and consume their food, and we are paying the price for it with our health.

Insulin Like Growth Factor 1 (IGF-1) is a normal part of all milk. This hormone is considered to be a fuel cell for any cancer. The medical world says IGF-1 is a key factor in the rapid growth and proliferation of breast, prostate, and colon cancer, and they suspect that most likely it will be found to promote all cancers.

Each bite of hard cheese has *10* times what's in a sip of milk because it takes *10* pounds of milk to make one pound of cheese. Each bite of ice cream has *12* times, and every swipe of butter has *21* times what is contained in the fat molecules of a sip of milk. Those nations with the highest dairy consumption also have the highest rates of osteoporosis.

Eighty percent of the protein in milk is casein. Casein is a powerful binder, a polymer used to make glue. It's better used to make sturdy furniture or hold beer bottle labels in place. It is in thousands of foods as a binder listed as caseinate. Casein is a powerful allergen, a histamine that creates lots of mucous. Dr. Campbell says that in multiple, peer-reviewed animal studies, researchers discovered that they could actually turn the growth of cancer cells on and off by raising and lowering doses of casein, the main protein found in cow's milk.

Grain

Grain Brain, written by Dr. David Perlmutter, shows the link between too many carbohydrates, including wheat, with inflammation and impaired brain function. I always test on my own body. I love rice, but when I eat it for dinner my hands swell which is my reminder that my tolerance level for grain is small. Since I removed most wheat and grain from my diet, brain fog is gone. Check out these ideas with awareness to see how your body tolerates different foods.

Adding

Victoria Boutenko, author of *Green for Life*, introduced this concept when she visited Calgary and shared her innovative green smoothie. The crowd of hundreds even got a delicious sample. We usually have to give up things we enjoy when we change our eating habits. Victoria suggested we add something high in nutrients to take some of the pressure off making a change.

My former husband Carl and I began drinking smoothies with hemp seeds, flax, spirulina, various other superfoods, and fruit more than ten years ago; it was suggested by the Centre for Integrated Healing in Vancouver. We spent time there when Carl was diagnosed with major illnesses. But Victoria took smoothies to a whole new level with her research on the vital nutrients and protein in greens, especially spinach and kale. Turning them into a smoothie makes greens easier to digest and to assimilate the nutrients.

Adding a smoothie for breakfast or lunch was an incredible boost and a big shift in our lives. Finding a powder with super foods can also help. It takes time to change and it can be overwhelming. Adding a nutrient dense food is a great way to shift by *adding* instead of taking away; and it can be easier to make better choices when we feel satisfied.

I am proud of my younger sister Janice for her innovative ideas. She has been involved in some aspect of the health industry since she was a teenager. She created a line with five nutrient dense powders under their company name Thrive from Eagles Song Health and Wellness on Whidbey Island, WA. More and more local stores are carrying their products.

Her husband Tom loves to teach the art of making smoothies and offers samples at health stores. Smoothies changed his life and helped get him off all his prescription meds. People often return to the demo table to buy a bag, reporting that the sample drink already made them feel better. Headaches disappear, and noticeable changes can happen in minutes. One customer who just re-ordered reported lowered blood pressure and help for his liver, and because of his success, his two siblings are now taking the products too. For more information see eaglessongthrivecafe.com

A well-known herbalist told Janice not to eat raw greens. "They will kill you," she stated several times. But raw greens have been a daily mainstay in my family's life for years with great results. It is important to let go of absolute truths about food and how it affects us. We are all different. We must trust our bodies as we find our own way.

Avoiding

Avoiding fake substances masquerading as food is important. This includes anything listed as low fat, sugar free, and diet. Read the label to see what is actually in the concoction. Remember that there are 10,000 ingredients that do not have to be listed as they are GRAS (generally recognized as safe).

Avoid margarine and oils like canola, safflower, and vegetable. According to Dr. Joseph Mercola, an alternative medicine proponent and osteopathic physician, margarine really is one molecule from plastic. It takes time to research and find our way and we must be smart about where the information is coming from. Our bodies need healthy fats for peak performance. My regular choices include coconut, olive, sesame, and almond oils and occasionally a small amount of organic butter. We need good fats, which help our bodies normalize and often excess weight drops off.

Sugar is best kept to a minimum. I prefer organic raw sugar or honey if I am using a little. We know these sweeteners are best in small amounts but at least their effects are known. The wide range of sugar substitutes is a mine field. Their effects are not known. We are the guinea pigs testing them. Avoid Splenda and Sugar Twin, and especially anything with high fructose corn syrup. These are cheap, very sweet products that mess up your metabolism. Instead, switch a recipe to use dates, raisins, ripe bananas, or other natural fruits for a little sweetness.

Avoid sugar free. Sugar free continues to shift to new chemicals once a current favorite, like aspartame, is shown to be detrimental. Once again, I rely on Dr. Joseph Mercola, a former osteopathic physician and well-known pioneer who helps educate the general public. You can easily find his reputable reports on the issue of sugar free and also high fructose corn syrup, the hidden ingredient in many sweet foods, and its detrimental effects.

I remember observing my co-workers nearly twenty years ago. We all had jobs in customer service sitting in front of a computer. When diet sodas and diet foods emerged, many of my heavier co-workers began to partake of them. How fascinating that they not only gained weight, but their bodies changed. They took on a flabby, obese form that was strange. This is what happens when a chemical sweetener messes up metabolism. I chose to ride my bike to work most days to balance that stagnant sitting job.

Also avoid gluten free. Once again, check the labels and notice how you feel when you eat it. Gluten free is usually cheap starchy flours that spike your blood sugar. I feel *off* for a few days when I eat them and my old addictive behavior kicks in. If your diet includes a lot of bread, it calls for a lifestyle change, not just switching to gluten free and eating the same number of sandwiches.

It is essential to read labels. Yes it takes time. When shopping with my children, we agreed on a rule. If the label had more than two or three things we could not pronounce, we did not buy it. That made Count Chocula, and other pretend foods, out of bounds. My children would read the label and put it back.

I used to buy Breyers Vanilla ice cream many years ago. The ingredients were milk, cream, eggs, vanilla, and a couple of things to stabilize it. We ate it as a treat with our birthday cakes and desserts. One day I had the thought to read the label again. To my surprise, it had the same ingredients as cheap, low quality ice cream. They lost my business that day, and I learned they were purchased by a large corporation known for highly processed foods. It is a great investment in time to read labels, but it's even better to buy foods with no ingredient list. Big corporations often purchase smaller companies that have a good track record for healthy ingredients, resulting in the quality going down; this was the case with Breyers.

Little Things

Little things all add up. We absorb from our environment, so be aware. Choose simple soaps, made locally if possible, and use white vinegar and soda for cleaning. Most anything can be cleaned well with simple, non-toxic, homemade solutions and elbow grease.

What we bathe in, clean our homes with, and put on our bodies is best when it can be food grade or as clean and non-toxic as possible. Sometimes people are obsessed with organic food yet their cupboard is full of toxic chemicals for disinfecting their homes.

I was one of them when I used to color my hair. This chemical concoction is regularly used by women and men of all ages. There are less toxic ones available such as henna. I was slathering the toxic stuff on my head every two weeks to cover the gray, because my hair grows quickly. I saw my incongruent behavior and had an awakening. I had been focused on eating healthy food and having a clean environment for years. Yet I was still willing to slather chemicals on my head and let them soak in. It took some time to adjust but I love my natural beautiful hair color.

Microwaves are one more little thing. Although the food that comes out of them does not kill you on the spot, it gives it the wrong spin which makes digestion difficult. We can easily see that the food is destroyed when it emerges. We all make choices in every moment. A pot on the stove has always worked if I want to warm up a meal. I have never owned a microwave and seldom use them. It is possible to make other choices that do not include its use.

If I am going to buy something to go on my lips or my skin, I often think, *can I eat it?* It will soak into my body through my skin, so if I would not eat it, I usually do not buy it. Once again, label reading is essential. Take the time, for you are worth it.

When I found vegetarianism and later veganism, I thought I had found the key to good health. And I had, but only for myself. We each must find what works for us by listening to our own guidance from our bodies. Whatever we choose, get the best, cleanest, highest quality possible. Our bodies know what to do with real food and we have decisions to make on the use of any processed food. Yet to have flexibility and feel freedom with our food choices leaves more space for joy and inspiration with our meals. How we feel is the key and if we are not satisfied, we can choose again.

SIX

Choosing Daily Practices

Every time you are tempted to react in the same old way, ask if you want to be a prisoner of the past or a pioneer of the future.

~ Deepak Chopra

I am delighted to share my favorite daily routines for your consideration. I simply practice what resonates and what works for my body. I trust you will do the same. We all have different needs at different times, so take what you like and leave the rest. I get up early and give myself a few hours. I truly love this gift to me for it sets my day up in a way that cannot be put into words. This was not possible when I was a busy wife and mother. But now as an Elder, it is my commitment to myself. If you are an Elder, think of this time as a redevelopment of your talents and your body.

These practices are free or low cost, which make them available to all of us. Self-love, discipline, mindfulness, and dedication to improving our well-being are needed more than money. Day by day we open to see that there really are no limits. It has been my true inspiration to discover areas to expand and evolve that I could not have imagined were possible. Health allows us to create the life we want, and no amount of money can buy it.

It is health that is real wealth
and not pieces of gold and silver.

~ Mahatma Gandhi

Over the past five years, my well-being and radiance continue to blossom. I feel youthful and strong with sustained energy levels which I love. I am always learning and growing, and I am a magnet for wonderful new ideas. I believe health is for us all. It requires time, commitment, and consistent practice, like anything we want to improve whether it's playing a musical instrument, swimming, or cycling. If an older person truly wants to grow younger, they must think, act, and behave like a younger person, and eliminate the attitudes and mannerisms of old age.

Pay attention to your posture. Straighten up. Think about your posture as you go about your day. I hold a broom handle, with both hands close to the ends, and lift it up and over my head; I hold it behind my neck with my elbows bent for one minute as I breathe deeply. This exercise was given to me by a massage therapist to reverse dowager's hump. It hurt to start with, but it helped my body remember what it feels like to stand up straight and tall. This takes decades off our appearance.

> *Once you fully embrace the wonderful reality that you can indeed become younger in appearance, health, attitude and once you energize that reality with focused desire, you have already taken your first drink of the healing waters of the Fountain of Youth.*
>
> ~ Peter Kelder, *Ancient Secret of the Fountain of Youth*

We need desire, time and focus towards anything we want to improve. We also need to detox regularly, which is similar to a thorough cleaning of our house or car. Our inner environment needs that shiny clean feeling too. How special when our car or home is freshly clean. It all seems to work better.

I have been too shy to share some of my practices openly before now. But I feel confident since I've personally tested these practices, and my level of well-being has improved greatly. When we are informed, we can make good decisions, and I feel blessed to be able to share the ideas that have come my way. Using urine and plant medicines like cannabis are out of the closet now. I intend that we can all learn and grow from each other.

These 12 practices are my foundation, but it is not always possible to do all of them every day. I do the best I can and love myself for what I do. Over the years practices have come and gone, but below are the enduring ones that work for me. Most of all, I am kind and gentle with my body.

1. *Affirmations or joyful prayers*
2. *Tongue scraping*
3. *Oil Swishing*
4. *Urine therapy*
5. *Apple cider vinegar, lemon, or lime drink*
6. *Meditation*
7. *Toning, sound, laughter*
8. *Movement*
9. *Breathing*
10. *Morning pages and write where you are*
11. *Green smoothies and super food*
12. *Barefoot walking and nature*

Affirmations or Joyful Prayers

I create a loving environment to support me in unfolding the light that I am. It begins as I open my eyes and realize I have the gift of another day. I have heard that around the world a million people die each day, but I am alive. I say thank you from a truly full heart. I have one more day to walk upon our earth.

As I described in the Self-Love section of the Choosing Our Attitudes chapter, most days I begin with love and thanks to my bed for being so comfortable and giving me such a great sleep. I speak to myself. *Dearest Cori, this is a blessed day. You are alive! There is time for everything we have to do. The Universe is for me. I see perfection in every moment. Life loves me.*

Then I rise and make my way to the toilet. After my bathroom stop, I look at my eyes in the mirror I affirm my love and gratitude to myself. I offer my praise and thanks for a wonderful body that works so tirelessly every moment to keep me healthy. Find words that work for you, write them on a card and keep it on the mirror you look into.

Tongue Scraping

This is a simple and free ayurvedic practice. Special tongue scrapers are available, but I use a small stainless steel spoon that's easy to travel with. Our oral cavity is the main gateway to the mind and body. Maintaining it is critical to our well-being. Scraping removes foul smells and tastelessness. When your tongue is free of the scurf coating, it brings relish and invigoration. Your tongue is one end of your digestive tract, and your body works hard all night to deposit bacteria, toxicity, dead cells, fungi, and food debris on top of it.

I gently scrape seven to fourteen strokes from back to front, and I rinse the scurf off the spoon with each stroke. This practice not only respects and supports my body's work but improves my ability to taste and makes food more satisfying.

Oil Pulling

This 2000-year-old practice is traditionally done with one teaspoon, or up to one tablespoon, of sesame oil, but olive or coconut oil are both excellent. Oil pulling can be done at the same time as showering, or any morning kitchen tasks. It helps with dental health and detoxification as the swishing removes unwanted organisms from teeth, mouth, gums, throat, and sinuses.

DO NOT SWALLOW. Swish up to 20 minutes, but a five minute swish is better than none. Do not spit down the sink. Find a way to dispose of the oil, either in the garbage or outside in a suitable place.

Dr. Bruce Fife, author of the *Coconut Oil Miracle* states that regular swishing, besides improving breath and mouth health, clears skin, improves digestion, helps with weight loss, promotes normal sleep patterns, and helps kidney and liver function. Indeed, Dr. Fife found that it was helpful with almost any condition, and oil pulling cleared his persistent skin problems when nothing else would.

Urine Therapy

One day in 1995, a book on urine therapy—unheard of in most of the Western world—fell into my hands in a bookstore. What a revelation to learn that urine is incredibly healing, sterile, and is free to all. Big companies have used it for years as the active ingredient in all manner of body products for hair and skin. Urine is antiviral, anti-fungal, and antibacterial.

Urine is a by-product when the kidneys filter blood. First blood goes through the liver, where the liver pulls out toxins and poisons which become bowel movements. This filtered, cleaned blood then moves from the liver to the kidneys where excess nutrients are removed to bring balance, or homeostasis, to the body. Once again, urine is sterile and safe to use. I have been drinking my urine quite regularly since I learned about it. The toughest part is getting over the mental block about it. It is not advised to drink urine if taking any prescription medications as it can alter your dosage.

Our body always balances our levels of sodium chloride, or salt, and water. Plasma ultrafiltrate or urea contains nutrients, enzymes, hormones, vitamins, antibodies, and minerals. Urea is listed as an ingredient in many creams and lotions. I decided to use my own urea rather than some gathered elsewhere. It is the ultimate in recycling, which the earth does so well all around us.

I catch the midstream of my morning urine in a cup or jar that I keep in the bathroom. I drink most of it right away and rub some on my face, arms, or legs. Urine has been commonly used for centuries in India and China. Besides drinking it and rubbing my skin with it, I have used it with great success for wounds of all sorts. It is my traveling first aid kit. It is best to soak a cloth or paper towel with urine, the right size for the wound, and tape it on—ideally overnight, but any length of time is fine. I use masking tape or some kind that will not bother your skin.

A friend called for help when an electric screwdriver slipped, jabbing a screw right to the bone in the joint of his pointer finger. He was willing to try urine as the pain was so severe and he had heard urine could be healing. He wrapped it up with a cloth soaked in his urine and put a plastic bag on his hand to keep it from leaking out when he went to bed. He said the intense pain subsided shortly after, and by morning the redness and pain were gone. He continued to apply his urine, and within a few days his hand was greatly healed.

Another friend had such intense pain from athlete's foot that he was willing to try his urine as nothing else had worked. He used it as a poultice with soaked cloths on his feet at night, covered in plastic bags. He began to drink it daily and used it regularly in foot baths. It was incredible how quickly his feet healed.

I fell on concrete while cycling on a narrow road in Costa Rica and scraped a deep chunk of skin out of my knee. Locals were worried that the heat and humidity would cause it to get infected and warned me that it would not heal. But with my special first aid kit, it did. It took time but I still marvel at this precious and free gift.

I recommend an e-book called *The Golden Fountain*, by Coen Van Der Kroon with well-researched data. As well as daily drinking, fasting on urine only is a powerful healing modality, discussed in a later chapter.

Apple Cider Vinegar, Lemon or Lime Drink

Cleansing and nourishing, apple cider vinegar is a simple morning drink, employing the principles of fermentation. It contains a wealth of raw enzymes and beneficial bacteria, which are responsible for the majority of its health benefits. One tablespoon in a glass of water, with a little honey if desired, is the recipe I first heard from health guru Paul Bragg back in the 1970s. It must have the mother and good brands like Braggs will say so. This means it has been fermented. The benefits include: helps the body become more alkaline; lowers blood sugar levels—beneficial for those at risk for type 2 diabetes; helps with absorption of calcium for strong bones; and can help lower blood pressure, improve heart health, relieve digestive issues, support weight loss, and slow down premature aging of skin. I use it in Canada, but it is not available in many countries I travel to where apples are not abundantly grown. Half a fresh lemon or lime squeezed into a glass of water is my solution to clean and alkalize my body in countries where citrus is cheap, fresh, and abundant.

Meditation

I was introduced to meditation when I was 16. I am grateful to my brother Bob for bringing Transcendental Meditation to our family in a small northern town in Canada. From the outside, we likely looked like a regular northern family, but I have memories of my younger brother Bryan reading Lobsang Rampa books as a teenager. I no longer remember the name, as it was more than 50 years ago, but on the cover was an exotic looking man, his head wrapped in an ornate turban with a glittering red ruby in his third eye. It was a very mystical choice.

Meditation is beneficial but I do not advocate any particular style. It can be restrictive when there are too many rules. The idea that it can be done wrong may add rather than reduce stress. There are endless ways to meditate, including the walking style. We can't do it wrong. If you are sitting quietly, focusing on your breath when you remember, that is enough.

These days, I call on the Quantum Field, an extension of my own energy field. I ask it to refresh, renew, and heal my body. I see my body open and flowing, knowing it is 99.999 percent vibrating fields of energy. I feel connected and in the flow. There is no need to micromanage my body. It knows what to do. I just focus gently on my breath and allow.

Meditation can be a chance to sit or walk, give focus to your breath, pay attention to your body, and feel the nourishment your breath provides. Breath is the difference between being alive or dead. That alone gives it utmost importance. Meditation is quiet listening. If you want to try a mantra, any word can be used. Sometimes my hands in warm water washing the dishes can be my meditation.

Tom Evans, author of *The Authority Guide to Mindfulness* suggests *Be* on the in breath and *Calm* on the out breath. Meditation completely changed Tom's life. He offers a free ten-minute meditation on his website. I love Tom's point of view, for he keeps it simple and doable. www.tomevans.co

Meditation benefits include: feeling more relaxed with reduced stress levels, becoming more tolerant of situations, mind expansion to new levels of capacity, and increased creativity and productivity. After time, we may look back on who we used to be and wonder how we got so stressed; we awaken our fully alive powers and become a force for change and transformation in whatever endeavor we apply ourselves to.

Sound—22 Minutes, Toning, Chanting, Drumming, Laughter

Many of us have blocks to freely opening our voices. I certainly did, but chanting in the Hawaiian language in the early nineties released that block. Chanting is for everyone. It is not singing. It's about breath, about heart, and about Spirit, and we all come fully equipped to participate.

Years ago, while living in Guatemala, an experienced sound healer suggested that making some kind of sound for a 22 minute time frame daily, would be life changing. We learned to use tuning forks and simple chakra toning. Sound changes us. It does not matter what sound we make and no singing ability is needed. One powerful sound is *OM*. Divide it with half *Ohhhh* and half

Mmmm. The power of your voice as it vibrates through your chest and nasal cavities can even align your chakras. Another simple sound is Ahhh, the sound connected with our heart chakra.

Because I love to drum and chant, that is often my morning routine. I do what I can in a myriad of different locations. I set my timer and go. Sound creates incredible patterns in sand which allows us to see the invisible patterns we are creating throughout our bodies. Our own voice is the most important healing sound for each of us. In my drumming-chanting circles, I encourage everyone to offer their own voice as a gift to themselves. Nothing moves our inner world like our own loving voice. Laughter is a great choice as part of the 22 minutes of sound. I look for reasons to bring the lightness and healing of laughter into my life as often as possible.

Movement—Kum Nye, Yoga, and Five Rites

It may sound funny, but the best kind of movement is the one we actually do. I love dancing, Zumba, walking, hiking, cycling, and yoga, but now my foundation of energy and strength emanates from Kum Nye. I love combining my own dance movements with chanting music as I stretch and deeply feel the music which invigorates my body.

In the early 1990s a friend from India gave me a book called *The Ancient Secret of the Fountain of Youth*. What a lovely inspiring gem, by Peter Kelder. I felt so strong and clear practicing the five rites outlined in this book. But many years later, I was injured in a head-on car crash. I was only able to do the first rite due to a fractured sternum. I stopped my regular practice and did some of it sporadically. Losing my upper body strength was huge as I have always been strong.

Know whatever comes to you unexpected to be a gift from God, which will surely serve you if you use it to the fullest. It is only that which you strive for out of your own imagination that gives you trouble.

~ Unknown

Three years ago, another Tibetan program called Kum Nye found me. Once again it was a gift of a book. Kum Nye was the answer to get my upper body strength back. The lovely book written by Stephanie Wright is called *Kum Nye, Waking Up for Beginners.* Stephanie is a chiropractor in London, England, and her book is truly a gift to the world. The eight positions described offer a complete body, mind, and spirit workout.

It takes time to build up strength for the eight poses. Each one is practiced for at least a week before the next one in the set is added. It took me four months to be able to complete a version of all eight poses in which each one is held for up to two minutes. But I kept going because I could feel the difference. Now I am strong with whatever I choose to do. I love that I can take it with me when I travel and practice wherever I am.

When I attend fitness classes like Zumba, I can keep up like a regular; two weeks after getting my bike out this spring, I rode 30 kilometers out to a nearby lake; walking up hills in Guatemala, much younger people asked me how I keep fit; I was easily able to walk 2.7 kilometers to a remote cacao farm when the roads were washed out due to rainstorms, pulling my suitcase, with my backpack full, and carrying my drum. Kum Nye is my foundation to health and vitality that takes less than twenty minutes to perform.

I include a one- to two-minute shoulder stand at the end of

Kum Nye just because I love it, and it contributes to my wonderful memory by opening more blood flow. I also practice 21 Spins, the first Rite of the Five Tibetan Rites. This affects each of the seven chakras, and stimulates hormones that regulate all of the body's functions. Our chakras are meant to spin at a high speed, and all at the same rate of speed, for perfect health. When one or more slow down, aging and physical deterioration set in.

When I began the spins more than 25 years ago, I could only do four or five spins. But within weeks, I was able to spin a full 21 times. I had no idea it would cure lifelong motion sickness. As a child I had to take a pill before any car trips so my parents did not have to pull off the road and let me out to vomit. Even as an adult, bumpy planes, riding in boats, riding backward in a car and not being able to see the road, would give me extreme nausea and a trapped feeling. I am excited to say I no longer have motion sickness. What freedom to move beyond those old patterns.

Breathing

I am no expert in breathing techniques, except that I have been successful with it, moment by moment, for over 66 years! I focus on it mindfully when I think of it through the day. I take a pause for three minutes every three hours and just breathe mindfully. This is part of a Gene Keys preparation for the Seven Sacred Seals program. Whatever kind of focused breathing you do, just find one you like and work with it. Air is our life force and the more we can get into our daily routine, the better our lives will be. Decide you will breathe mindfully at red lights, or at another time that fits. Feel the gift of life filling your lungs and be grateful.

Each morning I go outside to breathe in a special way. I learned it from a young Ecuadorian shaman named Nantar. It brings the focus of life force from the breath directly to our brain. I cross my arms over my chest with the left one on top, and I hold my ear lobes with thumb and pointer finger. Taking a big breath in through the nose while standing, then going into a squat on the outbreath gives a rush of energy directly to my brain. This is done 14, 21, or 28 times breathing deeply on the rise and out on the squat. Then seven rounds with my arms circling wide opens the energy and feeds my whole body. Then I place my hands to my heart, send out love and gratitude for the gift of life, and share it with all in the cosmos. These few minutes make a big difference in my mental clarity, for which I am very grateful.

Morning Pages and Write Where You Are

I am grateful for Julia Cameron's book *The Artist's Way*. I did her full program twice and have written morning pages for years. Morning pages are stream of consciousness so I write as fast as I can without thinking about it in advance. It clears the way for many kinds of creative activities to flow. I write without stopping for 20 minutes and if there is nothing to write about I write that there is nothing to write about and keep on going.

Secondly, I began using Junie Swadron's, *Write Where You Are* when needed, daily if necessary. It is always my ace in the hole when I find myself resisting writing or feeling emotions that are blocking or hounding me; I simply sit down and write where I am. It is so simple that it can be overlooked for fancy things. But it is free, except for a little paper and ink, and it makes a huge difference in letting my life flow.

Potions and Superfoods

Get as much of your nourishment from real food as possible. Our bodies know how to work with and break down food. We never know with any made up product. Trust your intuition and how you are reacting. It has been said for years that many bottles of supplements just go down the toilet and provide little or no value. You will know if a superfood is right for you by the way you feel. Adding in one thing at a time allows you to make a clear decision. I lost respect for some health providers when I saw 15 or 20 bottles of different substances that were sold to patients, like my mother. How can our sacred bodies make sense of that?

My favorite potion (food) for at least ten years has been a green smoothie. It is often my brunch. Starting with fresh greens of any sort (kale, beet, radish or carrot tops, lettuce, spinach) fruit, hemp seeds, spirulina or chlorella, turmeric or ginger. It is so versatile as any greens, fruit, or superfood can be used. I enjoy foraging for dandelion, thistle, nettle, or local and fresh ingredients wherever I am in the world. Nature provides for us if we look. There are many superfood powders on the market, so experiment but we always know fresh is brimming with life.

A powerful blender is great to make a green smoothie. However I have purchased kitchen gadgets that were only a fad. Thus I used an ordinary blender for two years before making the leap to buy a top notch one. It has paid off, for it makes a lovely smooth drink no matter what I put in. I often add chia or flax, or I use what I have available or what my body needs. The options are endless. I also add cacao beans either in the blender or as a garnish.

I have cacao in some form most days. Cacao is the bean chocolate is made from. It is not sweet at all, but it's loaded with nutrients, antioxidants, good fats, and magnesium; it makes a delicious drink by itself or forms the basis of truffles or energy bars. I use whole beans, pieces, or paste (ground whole beans).

For three years, my daily foundation is green algae called Bio Superfood. The spirulina and other types of algae are grown in remote areas of Russia and have been extensively tested by the Russian doctor who brought it to the world. It is a high quality superfood, providing an excellent source of nutrients as well as antioxidants. It is perfect for travel since the small capsules do not need refrigeration.

I also take a few drops of iodine as a daily supplement. In her brilliant book, *Cellular Awakening*, Barbara Wren writes, "Iodine has long been linked to thyroid function, but in reality it is required by every single cell within our bodies. It is vital for correct brain development and maintenance." Since our thyroid is responsible for many important functions in our bodies, giving it a boost with nascent iodine works well for me. It also helps me adapt to different temperatures when I travel.

I always have a few things I am trying out. One of them is cannabis in tincture and oil forms. I learned to make both. My skin loves the addition of the oil to my face cream. I often take a few drops of cannabis tincture before bed. Cannabis is a beautiful plant medicine our earth provides. As an adaptogen, it goes where my body needs it and I appreciate the positive effects. Its potent healing power is becoming accepted in the mainstream world.

My other trial is drinking my own version of Bulletproof Coffee. I make it with freshly ground organic coffee, coconut oil, brain octane, cacao paste, and cinnamon. Brain octane is created from coconut oil, said to be eighteen times more effective at delivering caprylic acid to our brain. I originally used MCT oil but found brain octane much more effective for a third more the cost. Dave Asprey, the creator of Bulletproof, says this combination can help our bodies by "raising ketones, those fat-burning, brain-boosting molecules in your body."

My mental clarity is astounding. The adaptation I chose does not include grass-fed butter and collagen as suggested in Dave's version and still after six months the capacity I have to clearly remember is surprising. One cup and I rarely need other food until lunchtime. Dave used it to help his body shed many excess pounds when nothing else worked. Once again, we each decide what is right for us.

Barefoot Walking and Nature

I spend at least five minutes a day walking in my bare feet on the earth. This can be much longer if I have a grassy park or a beach to walk on. We benefit so much from earthing, which is covered more thoroughly in a later chapter. We need the energetic connection from our earth and most people do not get it due to constantly being in rubber soled shoes, which blocks the earth's healing energy. Find a way to get your bare feet on the ground, even sitting in a chair. Right now I walk in the backyard in the morning, enjoy the beautiful plants, and check to see what they might need.

We all need that connection with nature daily. Keep it simple. Find a place where you can kick off your shoes for at least a few minutes, and get those bare tootsies in the grass or the sand. It helps to prepare us to deal with a full schedule or to bring balance and calm after a busy day.

My practices continue to evolve. Yet there have been ongoing improvements in my health and clarity so I know my current practices are working well. It is my pleasure to share them with all who are interested, to inspire others to know it is possible to dramatically improve, not decline.

SEVEN

Choosing the Sacred

A Bishop was on a large ship heading for the new world when he overheard some talk about a tiny island inhabited by some hermits who were practicing some heavenly aspects of living. He convinced the captain to stop there and went ashore in a small dinghy. He spent the entire day there, instructing the three hermits in the correct manner of prayer. It was difficult as they were elderly and had trouble remembering the Bishop's words. Finally at the end of the day, they seemed to have memorized it all and the Bishop returned to the ship tired but satisfied with his day's work. The ship sailed off, but in the night the Bishop could see a light in the distance that was catching up with them and beginning to overtake them. He called up to the first mate—what is it? Just at that moment, he saw the glinting grey beards of the hermits, lit up as their faces were, with a light shining from above. They glided upon the water, their feet acting as skis. "We have forgotten your words. Teach us again." The Bishop bowed low before the hermits. "You do not need them. Please carry on as you were." The hermits waved and turned back toward their island home, moving swiftly along the ocean.

~ Tolstoy

What is sacred? We can become lost in dogma, special words, or chants, but in the end it is our pure intention that matters. Ceremony and ritual is beautiful and needed as long as we keep it in perspective, remembering there are endless ways to have a sacred experience.

Prayer

Did you grow up with prayer? It is beautiful to offer thanks or say grace of some sort before our meals. For me growing up, we always had lots to be grateful for, such as having a home and food on our table. But my mother had released herself from the tight hold the Catholic Church had on her life, and my father did not subscribe to any organized religion. I was so happy to try any church or organization I wanted, and I explored widely.

It feels so wonderful to offer a prayer of thanks or a song to acknowledge all of us being together, and be grateful for all that we have. It's such a simple thing to realize that having food to enjoy is a blessed gift. Some choose the type of prayer or grace they learned according to the church doctrine they embraced. It is all perfect. When it comes from our hearts, the words do not matter. Our intention does.

Prayers are perfect when we use our own words as they come from deep inside and are relevant to the experience, not memorized and used by rote. A useful understanding of prayer is to use words to give thanks, love, and gratitude for what we already have. We all have so much, and when we recognize and give thanks it opens even more flow of all good things.

Life

Life is a gift. We learn that in different ways. Sometimes the understanding comes with a life threatening illness or when someone close to us dies. Our perception rapidly shifts when we have a close call, feel our mortality and how fragile the thread is between this life and our transition. This experience can significantly and dramatically change our top priorities.

I had that experience in a collision where we went down a steep embankment in a 16 foot cube van to avoid crashing straight on. We could not avoid the collision as a truck came straight for us across the centerline, but our injuries were minimal. Our lives had been spared and words cannot express this awareness of the sacredness of life.

But what is sacred? The little things are sacred. The sacred is in everything when our eyes are open to see. Nature is sacred, showing us perfection in every direction. How do we choose to see?

Vision

Some of my friends are sightless, or blind. I use the latter term because these friends helped me understand different ways our world can be experienced, for example, accurately *feeling the energy* of colors. I appreciate having vision with my eyes to see the world. We can accept vision as normal and pay little attention, or we can see it as a sacred gift. We choose. Could this be an analogy of how we can miss the sacred? It can be easy to take things for granted if they just seem normal.

Breath

Can breath be sacred? It is normal and happens automatically, so focusing on your breath is not required to stay alive. One day, ten years ago, I saw breath in a new way as I sat with my younger brother in the hospital. We did not know how long he would live. He could not breathe and had a tube running through a hole in his throat, and he was hooked up to a machine that breathed for him. Spending every day for two weeks in the hospital and hearing that machine breathe for my brother caused my thoughts about breath to shift dramatically. I have seen breathing as a sacred gift since.

My children's father was unwell, hooked up to oxygen and housebound, which also changed the way I saw my world. Just to get up and walk outside or be able to run across the street is a miracle. It is a sacred gift our bodies offer us. It is a sacred gift to be alive and have the use of our whole body. I am not a runner but once in awhile I run across the street just because I can. This is the main reason to thank my body every morning for the wonderful job it is doing. This is an important step in mindfulness.

All 60 plus trillion cells in our bodies take direction from our thoughts, feelings, beliefs, and words all day long. As the director, we must be aware that our bodies work better with praise and gratitude for a job well done than they do with criticism. Any employee does a better job when appreciated.

We are telling our cells how to respond all day long. Let's be aware of belittling comments. These are often couched in humor such as: I'm having a senior moment or what can you expect, I'm getting old. Listen for these comments accepting degeneration as a given in the aging process. Let's inspire our bodies instead with an open door to possibilities.

Many people in my life do not realize how sacred their health and full use of their bodies are, until they lose them. Sometimes we think enough money can buy our health back. Most often our health is not for sale at any price. This makes our bodies sacred miracles to be cherished.

Nature

I look out in my yard and see the miracle of all that is growing.

The little plant in the corner was only a foot high when I planted it this spring, and now it is up to my shoulder. Some are there for the beauty their flowers and greenery add to the world. Some of them feed the tiny creatures. Some of the plants—like kale, strawberries, mint, and basil—feed me. Their growth is a miracle. Awareness opens our eyes to see. The simple act of stepping on the grass with my bare feet is a sacred connection to Lady Earth, my term of respect for our Earth.

When we choose to see our lives and all life as sacred, it changes everything. I just returned home from Xenia, a special retreat center on Bowen Island in British Columbia. There, a Douglas fir named Opa has been alive and growing for over 1000 years. To sit on the wooden bench across from Opa, and think of all he might have experienced, made me wonder about our existence. So much is happening all around us that we will never know. This is the ebb and the flow of the miracle of life. Sometimes we just need to let go into the Mystery. And Xenia is quite the place to find peace, silence and deep relaxation.

First Nations people would honor the sun and the new day in the morning with a song. They knew that the sun was sacred. It was necessary, as was the rain, the rivers, and the lakes, for without them life will not happen. A sailor knows the cycles of the moon, for it affects the movement of the tides and his very existence.

Our systematic disconnect from nature or our source has happened gradually. We have busy lives that do not allow us the time and space to connect and contemplate with life. Often there is no time or space to grow our own food so it comes from a supermarket. We turn on a tap for water, or we buy it from a store. Choose to take a few minutes every day to really see and honor the sacred source of our existence. Even when research shows that being in nature reduces stress, the average American still spends less than 5 percent of their day outdoors. The average young person spends less than one hour a day outside.

Huna

Huna training in the early nineties on the Big Island of Hawaii taught me so much about the wisdom of the ancient people and their powerful connection with nature. Part of our work was to connect with the elements, one at a time. I took my notebook and sat by a pool of water. To sit and observe and simply be with the water as a sacred part of our existence was new for me. We create our own connection to life since we are all unique people. I felt the water in me connecting with the water in the pond. Symbols came to mind and I sketched them in my journal, helping deepen my connection and understanding of water.

We learned how the ancient Hawaiian people worked with the elements so closely that they could move impossibly heavy stones into an upright position. Their connection opened them to what we would call miracles.

We had several experiences of working in groups as four of us lifted a fifth team member. When that fifth person connected fully with earth element, we could not lift them. When they connected fully with air element, we could lift them with our fingers.

Medicine Wheel

Embarking on a shamanic path with Medicine Wheel teachings from South America, and later North America, brought me further along in seeing all life as sacred. I never kill anything. Even a fly or a wasp is respectfully removed from the house if they get in. Spiders as well as bees are gently taken outside. We choose how we interact with life in every moment. However, it is extremely difficult in our world to never kill anything for even the act of walking kills or damages life that we do not see. The way we eat contributes to this, as do the clothes and accessories we purchase. But instead of feeling guilty about it, can we choose to be aware and mindful and just do our best each day?

Homework for Medicine Wheel training was creating a relationship with fire. A student must learn to efficiently build a transformational healing fire and host a full moon ceremony. At first it was my own learning, but gradually 10 to 15 people gathered for a monthly full moon, sacred healing fire, and drumming circle. I learned so much about myself with fire as my teacher, culminating in an ongoing respect and love for fire.

There were rainy times when we had to cover the fire pit and the wood did not want to burn. This is all part of the learning. This foundational experience while hosting ceremonial fires gave me so much. But we do not have to rely on an experience once or twice a month, or even going to church once a week. The sacred is around us all the time, in every moment.

Ceremony

Choosing to see our lives and the world as sacred makes it so. Do you long for a taste of the sacred? There is a hunger for ceremony, ritual, and lives that have meaning. Making the choice to see our lives as sacred and as a miracle will give us the eyes to see. When I host ceremonies, I see how deeply participants drink in the taste of the sacred or the Divine.

Drumming circles have been an ongoing source of sacredness for all who attend and for me. These circles began in 2005 and have expanded into ceremonies around the world where we share a love of drumming and chanting, sometimes paired with the gentle plant medicine cacao which opens hearts. I hold space for earth honoring ceremonies of all sorts.

I have had the desire for years to experience a Rite of Passage into life as an Elder. I envisioned it as a sacred event with a ceremony. Finally, I realized it was my vision and thus my task to bring the idea forward because no one else was going to do it. I heard Marianne Williamson speak of a ceremony into the Elder chapter of life in an interview. She spoke of a book she had written containing ceremonies. I found her book and realized the context and words were not right for me, bringing home the understanding to create our own ceremony with our own words.

We claim our Rite of Passage ourselves, when we are ready. It is not bestowed upon us by another. The Elder chapter is a time to stand tall and show up with honor and respect for ourselves. Let's embrace and claim the Elder chapter of life rather than avoid it. Let's give value to our lives by grieving what we may have lost and celebrating who we now are.

The first honest step is being real. We all have fears about aging such as staying afloat with rising expenses, depleted savings, isolation, lack of a support system, and more. This happens at any age, but we free ourselves, especially in the Elder chapter of life, when we are willing to take *response-ability* or have the ability to respond. Our feelings and fears are a common thread among us all.

It is exciting to hear of others called to create their Rite of Passage. Angelyn, who owns a retreat on an island near Vancouver, was inspired by her daughter to stand tall and honor the Elder chapter she was moving into. When she turned sixty, she invited friends and family to the large ceremonial yurt on her property for a special evening of connection in her unique way.

Now I share with you, the way I created my ceremony, simply as information. I included some highlights of my life as well as my declaration going forward.

Rite of Passage as an Elder

This year, in July, I created my Rite of Passage as an Elder. I chose a full moon day called Guru Purnima, considered the most powerful day of the year in India. My intention was to align with the energy of that day as a beacon or a clarion call for all who are ready to claim Elder status. This is our moment. We know it for ourselves when we are ready to claim this Rite.

I began with gratitude for my two sisters of the heart, Nola and Karla, who came to support and witness me. The afternoon was hot so shade on the lovely deck surrounded by greenery was perfect. We stood and held hands as I opened sacred space, calling on my angels and guides with a special honoring of the elements. I spoke of other sisters whose hearts and support were with us, though they were unable to personally attend.

The three of us sat at a pretty round table. We talked of life as women and how this Rite fits in to honor the major phases of life. Karla inspired us with her vision of shifting the image of the Krone. She sees her as a beautiful wise woman of the forest, earthy and fully connected to nature, using the abundance of Medicine there. Karla intends to create a photo shoot on that theme.

A Rite of Passage as an Elder is for both men and women, but that warm day three women gathered. We had fun talking about our lives now and agreed how vital it is for women to meet and support each other.

I spoke casually about my life, which has been rich and adventurous for 66 years. I recalled growing up in a large family with six siblings. Married at 19, I had a complete life change. I was raised in a small town and marrying a farmer meant a move to the country. I had the privilege to be a stay at home mother, raising our three children, growing huge gardens, and living close to nature. We raised and rode Quarter Horses from the time the kids were toddlers.

Taking on and overcoming challenges is part of life. Some big ones were: learning to operate huge farm equipment; driving three-ton trucks full of grain; starting a business growing mung beans and alfalfa sprouts to supply stores in nearby cities; bringing aerobics classes to our little community complete with my own choices of fun music and choreographed steps.

After more than 20 years, I moved on as a single mother and once again the challenges made me stronger; during those years I moved to the city, worked with clients, and led workshops in personal growth fields.

Many years later, my second husband Carl and I shared a deep spiritual connection. During our years together we built spirit drums, a Medicine Bundle, enjoyed touring by motorcycle, and hiking in the mountains. Now as a single woman again, I feel the power of choice and possibility to create my best life now.

As I stood before my friends, I could feel the power of claiming my life as an Elder and the words flowed through me:

> *Being an Elder has nothing to do with age and everything to do with claiming wisdom and respect. We know it inside when it's our time to embrace Elder status. We can create a whole new reality of what it means to age and know what a true privilege it is.*

I claim self-love, self-respect, and vibrant health. I say YES to sharing the best of my wisdom, my gifts, and my talents in service to humanity. As an Elder, I choose a new way forward for I see a bigger picture.

I choose to be the change I know is possible and needed in our world. I know change begins inside first and radiates out, so I choose to redevelop my talents and skills and rediscover myself.

As an Elder, I choose to stop sidestepping what I know is true. My voice is needed and I have much to offer. But I must stand tall for my society calls me a senior. The status quo says I am old and will likely be feeble, incapacitated, and unable to care for myself. But that does not have to be true.

As more of us claim a healthy, wise, active, and keen Elder status, this will shift the paradigm on aging. A few Elders have shown us health, freedom, and a unique style well into their 90s. They have demonstrated what is possible for all of us.

I claim my new Elder status rather than have it bestowed upon me. I stand tall and add my love, wisdom, and voice to the world. I choose to take response-ability *for my own life and let go of blaming my childhood, or any aspect of my past. I choose to move beyond the space of a victim at the mercy of the system. I claim my power, freedom, and value.*

Elders are a vital and missing link that only we can recapture. Our skills and talents can be reclaimed. We can bring the simplicity, balance, and strength of knowing all is well, for we have lived through many challenges and can offer a mindful, slower pace.

With my strength, tenderness, and belief in Unity, I hold space for this beautiful new world we are creating together. I agree to BE present and open to the new possibilities unfolding. I live each day with gratitude for the gift of being a long-living woman, *a female Elder. I choose and claim radiance, freedom, wonderful health, laughter, and fun in my life.*

This sacred gift of living long cannot be understood until one reaches this chapter of life. I claim this profoundly rich and juicy time. All of my experiences and life events have created the Elder I am today and I step confidently forward to enjoy dessert, the sweetest chapter of life.

My friends' broad smiles and nods of encouragement were with me as I spoke. When I joined them at the table, they had generous praise for my vision. This ceremony ended as we moved to the shady backyard where we set our feet on the cool grass and shared a refreshing drink.

EIGHT

Choosing Healing Modalities

Natural forces within us are the true healers of disease.

~ Hippocrates

We have endless options for healing. Natural healing has been in place worldwide for millennia. The role of healing in Western medicine has been taken over by powerful corporate interests. In fact medicine is fairly new, only 200 years old. When we are in partnership with our bodies rather than treat them like the enemy that we must drug, cut, or burn, a whole new world opens up. It is wonderful to consider healing modalities as prevention before you ever need them. Our life is a holistic composite of all we experience. Let's begin with the most simple and free steps to healing.

Gratitude

A team of researchers from an Indian University recruited 43 participants who were suffering from anxiety or depression. During the first three sessions of their weekly counseling, half the group received an exercise—writing letters of gratitude to people in their lives for 20 minutes; the total time spent on this exercise for the week was one hour. It was up to the participant whether or not they chose to send the letter.

The other half of the group simply attended their counseling sessions without a gratitude task.

The study results show that "The participants who'd completed the gratitude task not only reported feeling more gratefulness two weeks after the task than members of the control group, but also, months later, showed more gratitude-related brain activity in the scanner. The researchers described these 'profound' and 'long-lasting' neural effects as 'particularly noteworthy.'"

Gratitude tasks work partly because they have a self-perpetuating nature. The more you practice gratitude, the more attuned you are to it and the more you enjoy its psychological benefits.

In other research, a gratitude practice by participants produced sustained reduction in perceived stress by 28 percent, and depression by 16 percent. Feeling gratitude is related to 23 percent lower levels of the stress hormone cortisol. Writing a letter of gratitude reduced feelings of hopelessness by 88 percent in suicidal patients. Gratitude is related to a 10 percent improvement in sleep quality and chronic pain.

Harvard researchers found that something as simple as writing down three things you're grateful for every day for 21 consecutive days, significantly increases your level of optimism, and it holds for the next six months. Gratitude is amazingly effective.

This simple act of gratitude has healing power. Have a gratitude journal by your bed to write three things from your day you are grateful for. To go to sleep with gratitude on your mind is powerful and free, and a process for at least twenty-one nights creates long lasting results. Write, paint, dance, or sing your gratitude as you let your creativity express the best way for you.

Gratitude helps cultivate a healthful mindset and physically changes our brain to encourage even more grateful orientation in the future. The more we recognize the good in life, the happier we'll be, leading to increased success overall.

Forgiveness

I first came upon this wonderful and simple exercise in 2006 when reading Colin Tipping's book called *Radical Forgiveness*. I used it a lot personally, felt like I had mastered the concept, and added it to my toolbox. I have offered simple workshops based on his teaching with the chance to fill in a worksheet and then discuss it or learn more about it. I travel with copies, even though they are free online on his website. I share them wherever I go when I meet someone who could benefit. Leading a workshop in Mexico, I talked about my own experience of using it when one of the guests was driving me crazy. Everyone enjoyed that I was so transparent as this particular person triggered many of us. That created laughter and fun. It was great proof for he became a new friend not long after I did the forgiveness worksheet. Find a free copy at www.radicalforgiveness.com

Forgiveness is a gift we give ourselves. It is not about the other person. We are each brewing the emotions we hang on to, like a stew in our belly. We forgive to free ourselves. Often, the most important person we need to forgive is ourselves.

Speaking to Ourselves

We are never alone. Sixty plus trillion cells are listening and responding to all our thoughts and words. We need to pay attention to and be mindful of our self-criticism and judgment. We clearly see that we get exactly what we order up. The quantum field, which is our body's extended energy, just gives us what we ask for, often unconsciously.

It is often easier to see and hear others than it is to see and hear ourselves. I asked a man I had not met who lives in the same complex for help to bring my bicycle home with his truck. He kindly agreed to do so. We exchanged names. Then he jokingly added, "I am the short, fat, almost tall guy in the complex." Wow. He described his short, fat body perfectly. His sixty trillion cells are doing exactly what he is ordering up—even though he doesn't realize it. Our cells just do what we tell them to.

So, let's be mindful and aware of what we say to ourselves. Choose affirmations with gratitude and praise for what is already working. Start somewhere and keep adjusting your words.

One of my favorites is simply *Thank You, Thank You, Thank You*. That is easy and never goes out of style. Thank you for my life, thank you for this day, thank you for my legs that work so well. Thank you for one more day to walk on the belly of Lady Earth.

Each day for many months I have been saying, *all of life is organizing in song around my success and I am very grateful.* After an intense writing period and a conversation with an editor, I went out to lie on the grass to balance out so much computer and phone time. As I lay down, dozens of little birds I had never seen before were chirping and trilling, flitting from tree to tree with such an unusual sound. Ravens flew overhead with their *berk* call, and shared the blessing of their swishing wings. I suddenly realized I was hearing the song that is organizing my success. How sweet.

I so appreciate my body and the gift of life. A few days ago I hopped on a bus to a nearby community on a lake with my bicycle. The cycling trail is a beautiful 30 kilometers through old forests. I began to notice and appreciate all the parts of me that were engaged in my cycling adventure. Each toe, foot, heel, calf, knee, thigh, hip, buttock, and my whole spine was engaged. Also my internal organs were part of the adventure, especially my heart and lungs, as were my hands, arms, elbows, shoulders, neck, head, eyes, and ears. I cycled along, aware of the miracle of my body and gave thanks to every part of me for working with such grace and ease. One tiny sore part would have kept me at home. We get great reminders with a little pain. It's great to be thankful and take nothing for granted.

Listening

Listening has always been a sacred act and a healing modality. When doctors, nurses, and other healthcare practitioners had more spacious time with us, their listening was a powerful healing act. Often gems emerge that illuminate the issue, simply when we listen. A young woman I met who was put on antidepressants said all she needed was some time and some caring. When she and her long-term boyfriend ended their relationship, and a good friend committed suicide, there was no one to listen and just be with her in her pain. A busy overworked doctor wrote her a prescription, and she slipped into the spiral of being half alive on medication.

Having someone listen fully, creates an opening for healing and change. This young woman had the courage to come off her medication. A therapist or counselor can be paid to listen. However we can learn to offer this gift of listening to each other. Especially valuable is full body listening with no advice. When we can listen, hear each other, and respect each other's own knowing, it changes everything. We all need someone who cares enough to take time to listen in this busy world.

One of my offers to community is from a book called *Speaking Circles* by Lee Glickstein of California. This circle creates a special focused way of listening to each other. One person speaks and the rest listen with their whole body, making soft eye contact. We feel the connection we all have through the earth and our hearts. Each person has the same number of minutes and is not required to speak but to simply be present for their allotted time. It is safe. There is no pressure or expectation.

This process allowed a wonderful breakthrough for me while in training in San Francisco. In my group of four, I caught myself preparing what I would say as others spoke. Of course, I could not really hear the one speaking, as I was too busy in my own world. I was afraid nothing valuable would come to me when it was my turn. I let go of that deep desire to be accepted and began to listen fully, trusting that I would have words. When it was my turn, I chose not to speak, which is huge because I am a talker. It was perhaps the first time I sat in silence for my four minutes and made eye contact with the three other women. There was no pressure to speak. We simply held each other with our presence. It was a beautiful moment.

Others at the circles I offered years later told me the experience of deep listening changed their lives. It is my preferred way to begin any workshop or presentation, for it creates a connection and a cohesive group, more than anything I have experienced.

Support of Community

The devastating effects of loneliness and isolation hold great importance in the holistic picture of our lives. It does not seem to be addressed much. People of any age and especially seniors can feel discarded or not valued. Deepak Chopra gives a brilliant analogy of how a culture is based on what we value. Our Western world values money, possessions, and status, so that becomes the measuring stick of success by the masses. The Russian people in Abkhasia value longevity above all else. So that culture is motivated to live up to it and celebrate *long living people*. And longevity is a gift to those who expect it.

I took a taxi to catch an early commuter bus one morning. The female driver said she had been with the cab company 14 years. She sadly related that many of her customers are seniors who take a taxi just for some contact and a place to speak to another person. What a powerful reality check. Isolation, loneliness, hopelessness, and helplessness all flow together. I see it in Elders who act like seniors in the complex where I am house-sitting; they become busy bodies nosing into other people's affairs just because they are lonely and seeking connection.

The healing power of a supportive community is essential to our health. We need others we can share with, in any meaningful activity. Especially good are uplifting groups where there is a focus on something positive like line dancing, walking, swimming, or cycling. Let's seek and create communities where people are keen and looking to grow, which keeps us fresh and expands our mental capacity. Groups where people routinely gather just to share their latest health crisis and try to outdo each other by comparing their war wounds and pain can be depressing. Choose wisely with your precious time. Let's create healthy communities where we can all flourish.

Developing Trust in Our Bodies

We may think we can control our bodies but they continue to be a mystery. It is invaluable to develop trust. Our bodies are miracles working every moment without our interference. My back issue detailed in chapter 4 is a great example. My body and mind, emotions and spirit working together caused a beautiful unfolding. Emotions came to the surface for balancing. The pain in my back was a humbling reminder of how powerful my body is and how it can stop me in a moment. It culminated in a revelation of deep understanding.

Traveling in Thailand in 2013, was another time of trust. The last day before we embarked on a boat journey down the Mekong River into Laos, we decided to rent scooters. A circle ride to Myanmar first, then the Golden Triangle—where Myanmar, Thailand, and Laos all come together was our plan. It was a sunny day and we each drove our own scooter, feeling true freedom. I loved the uniquely special energy at the Golden Triangle. We had a delicious late lunch in a Thai restaurant overlooking the Mekong River and relaxed in the warm breeze. The magical energy captivated us and we dallied too long.

I am not an experienced scooter driver and it was harder to drive in the dark. I was in the lead as we approached Chaing Rai and I took a wrong turn. We had to stop under a streetlight to read our map and realized our hotel was close. Suddenly exhausted, I lost control as I made a sharp turn and accelerated. Down I went, crashing into a construction zone. Moments later, Carl and Thai locals picked the scooter off me and lifted me out of the rubble. As a small group gathered, a young Thai woman beside me started screaming for she saw blood spurting out of my hand, soaking my light colored shorts. It was coming from a small cut over a vein in my right hand, and I immediately applied pressure to stop the bright red flow.

Locals wanted to call an ambulance, but I refused. I was fine. I could walk and the hospital was just a block away. I had seen it a few minutes before we stopped to look at the map. It was an easy walk, and thankfully one young Thai doctor on duty could speak English. They checked me in immediately and allowed Carl to stay with me.

My blood soaked shorts gave the illusion of a bad injury. The staff checked my whole body to find where the blood came from. I kept pointing to my hand but they did not understand until they washed it. We all started to laugh when they realized all the blood really had come from that tiny cut. A small bandage did the trick. They took x-rays to look at my wrist and arm, which hit the handlebars quite hard when I went down.

What a relief to find out nothing was broken. The doctor told me I would have to pay for the treatments and x-rays before I left. Included in the price (of less than twenty dollars CDN) were four prescriptions dispensed from the hospital pharmacy. I told him that I do not take drugs. He insisted that I should.

He told me that one was for pain, another for swelling, another was an antibiotic in case of infection, and the fourth was to help my stomach deal with taking the other three. What a reality check. When we cut our finger, we trust that it will heal and our body does its mysterious work. We do not micromanage it. The process is the same with tumors, illness, and my injured arm. My body knows how to heal itself, and I decided to honor that and just get out of the way.

I took one antibiotic. But my body said I would need the healthy bacteria in my gut for the rest of our five weeks on the road in Asia. This is not the time to kill them, I thought. I threw all the other pills out except the antihistamines, which relieved my swollen arm in the heat for the first three days. What a great lesson.

Earthing or Grounding

Can you imagine a therapy that can soothe and support every single organ in your body? It can boost your metabolism, stabilize your blood sugar, promote better sleep, and offer comfort. It is also the single best thing to protect your future health, is antiaging, and anti-inflammatory too.

This therapy is connecting with the earth, otherwise known as grounding. Physically touching the earth directly, with no shoes or rubber mats in the way, has been clinically proven through blood tests, imaging studies, sleep tests, and research to be an extremely powerful agent; it provides head to toe healing inside and out.

Dr. Mercola advises that this simple act, achieved by walking barefoot on the earth, transfers free electrons from the earth's surface into your body that spread throughout your tissues. Grounding is a potent antioxidant, relieves pain, improves sleep, enhances well-being, and much more.

I first heard of earthing when I watched a documentary called *The Grounded*. It was filmed in Alaska and the beautiful and true story is about how earthing healed a whole town. The concept of grounding, and its necessity for the health of all living creatures, makes sense when we consider how dependent and intricately connected we are with the earth.

Every time we take a breath of air or a drink of water, we are in essence connecting to the earth and using it for our very survival. Grounding is really one more extension of this; it's one more way we are intelligently designed to coexist as a part of nature.

I have been walking barefoot as much as possible my whole life, at least in the summer. I love it and feel it is part of the holistic picture of keeping me vibrant. It's a simple and free healing modality, so it makes sense to ground as much as possible. Over the last four years, living in Mexico, Guatemala, and Costa Rica, I walked barefoot all day, every day, whether on the grass, soil, stones, or sand on the beach. My feet were a little tender when I first started, so I took it slowly and only put on shoes to shop for food or other essentials in town.

One of my friends who lives in Costa Rica and is used to the relaxed barefoot lifestyle there, put a post on Facebook: He arrived at the airport in San Jose for his flight to the United States, looked down and realized he had forgotten shoes. As often as possible, I get my bare feet on the earth, even for a few minutes on a little patch of grass in the city.

Vision for Life

I have known our eyes can stay healthy and refused to buy into the need for glasses to read fine print. But I could not find the information I was looking for to really prove this and work with it. Then I found this brilliant book, *Vision for Life* by Meir Schneider. Born legally blind in Israel, Schneider tells his story of teaching himself to see. He documents his amazing success with an image of his U.S. driver's license as proof.

First, we have to become aware that it is possible to improve our vision. We have been programmed to accept wearing prescription lenses instead of doing what is needed to strengthen and improve our vision. We have been told the sun is dangerous and we must protect our eyes with sunglasses. Thus our eyes get deprived of the precious light they need to function. School and books and our lifestyle of computers and devices, where we use a small portion of our visual field, contribute to the issue.

We have to break out of that box or paradigm to know there is more possible. It is a holistic endeavor that affects our lives. I am happily using parts of the program relevant to my vision. One important daily step is looking far in the distance, ideally up at the sky, for at least 20 minutes. This balances up a lot of computer or book work and helps my eyes relax and restore. Schneider's programs are on YouTube showing simple, useful practices.

Miracle Mineral Supplement

I heard of Miracle Mineral Supplement (MMS) as a simple, inexpensive treatment to heal many terminal diseases. MMS was created by Jim Humble to help his group situated in Africa when they contracted malaria.

While at a standing-room-only lecture in a health store in Calgary, it was revealed that an Asian man helped his mother recover from a terminal diagnosis of cancer. I wanted to try it. Since prevention has been big my whole life, I like to try new things. I have used protocols to detox my body for most of my life. To me it is just like taking care of your home or car or cleaning your outer body with a shower or bath. Our insides need a good flushing too, like an oil change.

When I arrived at The Sanctuary in Mexico, Pete, the owner, offered me the general MMS protocol. He had taken training based on Jim Humble's criteria. Humble's research proved the elimination of many diseases such as malaria in days. How incredible that these simple therapies can be made suspect and wiped out by powerful interests. The public instead gets confusing information by design.

I learned how to mix the two components carefully and began with one drop every hour in a cup of water. It was easy and effective to mix all eight portions for the day in eight cups of water, and to drink one cup each hour.

I learned when we are detoxing, our bodies might create diarrhea if toxins need quick elimination. Daily enemas, at least when loose bowels struck, were a wise suggestion. I never thought of it that way before, but it worked.

I added one drop to the hourly dose each day, intending to get up to three drops every hour for the eight-hour period. I could only stay on that many drops for a few days and the detoxing made me feel tired and generally unwell. So I reduced the dosage to one drop every hour, and completed the protocol for the full 21 days.

This cleansing of parasites, fungus, and bacteria changed my body long term. I have been over my ideal weight most of my life and using this 21 day protocol created a noticeable shift. Adopting a vegan, gluten-free way of eating, my weight gradually changed and 40 pounds disappeared in the subsequent four years. I didn't diet or try to lose it. Instead, I eat as much as I want of beautiful plant-based and gluten-free foods.

Link: www.mmsdrops.com

Urine Fasting

It is disturbing to see so many people sick and going for the only therapies their physicians can suggest. There are many sites online for complete details of this powerful and free therapy also called uropathy. I have been shy to speak openly about it before now. And yet I strongly believe that we all need access to information, and we can each decide what to do with it. I came to the conclusion that it is wrong for me to keep my success to myself because of the fear of criticism.

I could never have imagined that several challenging conditions I was living with could be healed, so sharing this with others is my way of offering hope. Over the past five years, I have completed five fasts solely on my own urine and water. After my second fast, of nine days duration, I was delighted by the following results:

1. *Incontinence is gone. I lived with this for ten years and I did not dream it was possible. It has only improved in the six years since; I no longer dribble at all.*
2. *Many years of bowel upsets with loose stools and urgency in reaching the bathroom is very much improved; by 2016, my digestion was normal, I had healthy stools, and the urgency was gone.*
3. *My teeth and gums are healthy and strong, and I no longer experience bleeding gums.*
4. *The dull ache and pain in my body that made me want to stay in bed is gone.*
5. *The dowager's hump that was developing is almost gone, and I can now stand tall.*

I share my story to give confidence to those who might want to try the fast. But once again, the best source for your education is *The Water of Life* by J.W. Armstrong and it must be read several times to understand the process.

Urine fasting is completed by drinking all urine eliminated day and night, and sipping just a little cool water when thirsty. No food at all should be taken for success. Also, full body rubbing with urine aged three to ten days is essential. It takes about an hour at least once a day, which is no problem as that much time is saved by fasting. My comments here are solely for awareness and more education is needed for success.

My third fast was 19 days long. We lived in a large house in Alberta and my friend Anaya said she would not have believed it was possible if she had not seen me daily. We had a busy routine growing, harvesting, and preserving our own food so she was aware of my energy levels and knew I wasn't eating. I didn't lose much weight. I also kept my regular routine of leading two

Zumba classes weekly.

My own e-book *Fasting on Golden Elixir* contains details of my last nine-day fast and the overall effects from the five fasts I have completed over a five-year period.

Stinging Nettle

I gathered, dried, and drank this simple, inexpensive, and widely available herb daily for two years. It is recommended to: stabilize blood sugar, reset metabolic circuits to normalize weight, reduce fatigue and exhaustion, restore adrenal potency, lessen allergic and menopausal problems, and eliminate many chronic diseases.

An infusion is made by placing one cup of leaves in a quart jar, filling it with boiling water, covering and steeping the leaves for four to ten hours. Drink one to four cups daily. Refrigerate after steeping but only for two days. Nettle does so much for so little.

A herbalist who advocates nettle was close to needing dialysis; using the infusion daily, her kidneys were completely rebuilt. Nettle also extends and rebuilds the strand in our DNA called *telomeres*, which is responsible for longevity.

It is *the* herb for restoring kidney health, decreasing inflammation, restoring elasticity and tone to veins, helping keep blood pressure in a healthy range, and strengthening individual energy and immunity.

Nettle is loaded with bioavailable nutrients that restore health to every cell of the body. It contains all vitamins, except B12, and all minerals needed by the body. It tones and strengthens the kidneys, adrenals, lungs, intestines, arteries, liver, and circulatory system. Nettle's bioavailable iron enriches blood and counters tiredness. Hair and skin are the first to benefit. Energetic, hormonal, and magnetic fields are restored to vibrant health with regular use of nettle infusion.

Vibration Machines

Machines that change the frequency of our bodies have been around since the 1920s. Decades ago I was very interested to read Royal Rife's story about his success helping people heal cancer, and other potentially terminal diseases, using his device to shift their body vibration. His success attracted the attention of Big Pharma and he was stopped.

But devices continue to surface. In1990, I used and marketed a machine that helped people regain their health. Tremendous pressure is put on these companies when they have success and it got to be too much. In 2010, a different vibration machine emerged. With just ten minutes standing or sitting in various poses, I noticed my body changing, and I felt more vibrant and energetic. With my small portable machine, I became toned. My upper arms looked lean and muscular. There is now expanded information about the value of these machines and how they can help our bones and muscles stay strong with less effort. It does not substitute for regular exercise and movement. Family members and friends, both younger and older than I am, enjoyed the effects.

Using a vibration machine can substitute for use of weights. Research over fifteen years confirms that a number of direct effects on the body are possible including stimulation of muscle and other reflexes; mobilization of joints and muscles; increased muscle power; reduced warm-up time; increased energy; stronger bones and improved bone density; better agility; and improved flexibility.

Detox and Liver Cleanse

Since fasting, detoxing, and cleanses are huge subjects, it is wise to do your own research depending on your needs. I am not an expert but have derived benefits from these modalities my entire life.

I recommend a liver cleanse using the protocol of the Global Healing Center in Texas, U.S. They have been highly effective for me. Dr. Group worked as a naturopathic doctor for twenty years and saw the powerful effects of detox. He saw that detox was the first step in creating health for his patients. Dr. Group wanted to have a bigger impact worldwide and created the Center. His educational step-by-step online videos are excellent and the products are shipped around the world.

Using their protocols, I have completed six liver cleanses over a period of three years, and my health just continues to improve. I took pictures of the hundreds of stones my body eliminated as it was impossible to believe. They are posted on my website blog.

I make it a habit to work with people who are walking their talk. I want my healthcare provider to be radiating health. Forty years ago, my cigar smoking, overweight M.D. got a trade in for healthy practitioners of various kinds; I never looked back. We are all unique and need different things at certain times. It is best to leave the details of detoxing to Dr. Group's fine, informed staff and others you will find along your journey. Trust yourself. There is a wealth of education about fasting and detoxing on Dr. Group's website.

Link: www.globalhealingcenter.com

Hearing

Hearing loss is another area to examine. Is it just to be accepted as inevitable? I need a hearing aid. Are you sure? Does it really come with aging? Louise Hay's understanding is that we unconsciously create hearing loss when there is something in our lives we do not want to hear.

It is possible that ear candling can help. Using this simple technique, excess wax is drawn up and out of the ear and into a beeswax cone. The practitioner inserts the small end into your ear, while the large end is lit as you lay down on your side. It is incredible to see the beeswax cone fill up with rusty ear wax. It's undeniable when you see it for yourself.

We need patience to adjust after removal of the earwax, for ears affect our balance and equilibrium. Ear candling can be completed in about an hour and is worth trying before we accept hearing loss. I know from friends and family who use hearing aids that these devices often create havoc instead of harmony.

Find a therapist who offers ear candling. It makes sense to try this before thinking hearing loss is permanent and going forward with expensive, and not necessarily efficient, hearing aids. Of course this may be necessary in the end, but why not work with the emotional aspect and then give your body support and a chance to heal itself?

Informed Decisions

If we suddenly become sick with a scary diagnosis, it's hard to know where to turn. Friends describe the fear that kicks in. Feeling scared and pressured by family, as well as doctors, into the huge vortex of Western procedures is common. Exploring our options before the need arises helps us make knowledgeable rather than emotional choices.

When we have the courage to take the space and time, we can find many options. In truth, some conditions may need immediate attention. However, most diseases have been developing over many years. Taking a few weeks or months to make an informed decision regarding our sacred body is our right. Most of all, it helps to educate ourselves early.

If I received a diagnosis of a disease today, I would likely go on a two- to three-week urine fast. Then I would re-evaluate and perhaps stay on mostly vegetable juices, and I would use the healing power of cannabis oil. I would definitely get help to clear the emotional aspects that are always part of a disease. Dealing with the emotions, to free our bodies to heal, is essential. It is all part of the holistic package. But of course this is just what I would do for myself and we each have to make our own informed decisions for our own lives.

NINE

Choosing How We Die

Some do not understand that we must die.
But those who do settle their quarrels.

~ The Buddha

Death is the Great Mystery. We can ruminate about what happens when we die, but no one living can say for sure. It is so important to face death. To face and be willing to know death means we can really live our lives to the fullest. To push death away simply means a denial of this inevitable event. Denial does not change the inevitability of death, but it disempowers us. When we embrace it and begin to contemplate it, and live each day as a juicy exploration of possibilities, our life becomes richer.

Seek out others who have the courage to speak of death in useful ways. Death can be a beautiful thing. Although I cannot prove it, I know it is not the end for us. It is the end of our lives in our physical bodies on this planet. If you have ever been with someone dying, in a peaceful setting like a hospice, you might see it in a new way. It is possible that the passing of a loved one can be a holy, sacred gift depending on circumstances. We never know for sure what will come. But to get as comfortable with death as we can allows us to be a peaceful presence for others, and our lives may blossom in unexpected ways.

Awareness of death came strongly into my life around 1990. I decided to learn more about it. My husband and friends were not interested in discussing it or delving deeper. I felt drawn to become a hospice volunteer for people who were in the last stages of life, thus I was required to take a course called Death and Dying. Two nurses from the small local hospital taught the course, and it was phenomenal. An important part of the training is acceptance. As a volunteer, we agreed to be present and honor the beliefs of the individual and family members. We were not to push our own beliefs and ideas on others; we were asked to simply be present and open to what they needed. Just to be willing to listen is powerful, helpful, and enough.

I loved all I learned in the course. Then I was matched with a family whose mother was in the last stages of cancer. It was incredible to spend time with her. There is something so valuable in being able to talk to someone who can be real. Family and friends have an emotional attachment. It can be difficult to face that your loved one is leaving, but a trained volunteer can just be there for the family and the dying person. Being a volunteer was such a rich and deep experience for me. The family thanked me so much for being a neutral sounding board for them in the midst of such an emotionally vulnerable time.

Because of my openness about the topic of death, I seem to create a space where people can share safely. Some years later I moved to an area near Edmonton, in northern Alberta. My landlord was unwell. He was trapped in a motorized wheelchair since both legs were amputated stubs above his knees caused by circulation loss from diabetes. He and his wife loved to have me stay for tea and a visit when I came to pay the rent.

At one point, he said to me, "Are you reading my mind? How can you tell what I am thinking?"

"I don't have to read your mind," I told him. "I just listen to what you say and you tell me what is on your mind."

Then he openly admitted that he knew he did not have much longer to live, and he was terrified of dying in the winter and being put in the frozen ground. It is so therapeutic to be able to voice deep fears.

As we discussed death and what we each thought would happen, his wife told her story. When her mother died in Germany, she was in Canada and was unable to be with her siblings. But, she woke up seeing a vision of her mother the night she died. Her mother expressed her love, asked for forgiveness, and said goodbye. My landlord was stupefied, and asked his wife why she didn't tell him. She answered sheepishly, "Oh I don't know."

People often have no place to share these messages in our society. We can feel embarrassed if we are told it's just our imagination. We were encouraged, as hospice volunteers, to believe these stories. The nurses who provided the training told us that when people die, there is at least one communication with loved ones to let them know they are okay. But most often this gets ignored, as we have no place for these experiences to be honored as truth.

When my younger brother suffered through a long bout with cancer, it was tough on the whole family but especially his wife, Malou, and three young sons. When he entered hospital in June my siblings all came for a few days; I was fortunate to have more time. I stayed two weeks longer and spent time in his hospital room. He could not talk so he wrote out his comments with paper and pen. It was painful to realize I would likely not see him alive again. Life support helped him breathe through August, and then he moved into hospice care.

I was at a Shamanic training in the mountains in southern Alberta when my family sent me a message letting me know his time was close. The doctors in the hospice saw signs that he was ready to go when he pulled out his own breathing tube. I gave the family my blessing and said I would come as soon as I could. The course ended two days hence and I booked a flight east.

I awoke early the last morning of the course and set off hiking up the mountain. My brother was on my mind as he was such a keen hiker, cycler, tennis player, enthusiast of many sports, and a lover of life. High up in the Rockies were stunning views in every direction. I felt peace and gratitude with raw nature all around. Suddenly, the wind whipped up in a mini whirlwind. The leaves swirled around in a powerful gust. Then I heard his voice: "Sister, sister it's true. We have eternal life." Then the leaves swirled around in another powerful gust and were gone. I sat in the stillness and peace for a long time with gratitude for my brother's last gift.

In his late 80s, my father was hospitalized due to a few brushes with illness; after one such event he told me, "I wake up each day and open my eyes. I take a breath. Oh. I am alive. I have one more day." What a simple and profound way to live. We are gifted each morning with one more day. We choose how to see it, each day. The passing of a loved one can help us clearly see that life is a gift.

Dad said he wanted to die with his boots on, working his own land at age 95. He never wanted to be put in a facility where he would not know his own name, and need to be fed, bathed, and dressed. He chose to die while he was still active. Although his health had been failing a bit, he was still out working on the land.

He made plans to settle his affairs, put his land up for sale, and found a buyer. He died a few weeks later. He went into the hospital on a Friday, the family was called, and he died on Saturday. Who can complain about 89 very full years as a healthy, active sportsman, gardener, talented musician, and handyman, with two marriages and seven children? In fact he built the last home my parents lived in together when he was 70.

Through synchronicity, I met Melvy, a Mexican woman of Mayan heritage. I had lived in Mexico for five months when we met. Melvy was a woman who lived a rich life; she lived in California for 25 years while going to school to become a lawyer, and she spoke five languages. She raised a daughter, Lucie, and son, David, in California. Her more complete story as told to me is in her soon to be released book, *Touched By Angels.*

We met on a bus in the Yucatan. Melvy had been legally blind for eight years, and she had experienced many brushes with death from the time she was a young child. She taught me so much.

When Melvy was in her thirties, 15 years before we met, she was in the hospital on life support. Melvy heard the doctor telling her husband, Jose, she would not likely live until morning. Jose came into her room crying, and they prayed together. Jose loved Lucie and David and he was a good stepfather, but he was praying Melvy would be there to see them grow up.

One of the many miracles in her life happened that night. A light in the corner of her hospital room materialized into a wispy angelic shape. Melvy asked, "Are you my angel?" She thought it was the angel of death who had come to take her. "I am your angel but I am here for a very special purpose." The angel floated over to Melvy's bed and touched her forehead. Instantly her organs began to function again and the machines screamed in protest. The nursing staff came running and no one could believe what had just happened. Her doctor was called in. After two days of testing, she was released from the hospital. A fingerprint scar in the shape of a horseshoe remained on Melvy's forehead where the angel had touched her. All her friends and family knew it had not been there before.

A safe and comfortable place where we can explore ideas about death is called a Death Café. There, we are able to have rich and honest conversations. I attended my first one in Calgary, Alberta, a few years ago. Once again, none of my friends wanted to explore it with me. It is so real to talk about death. We are all going there sooner or later. Why not explore it in a place where others are also willing to learn together? It is a way to move beyond our fears and embrace the inevitable.

The Death Café was held in a University coffee shop. I felt deeply nourished for days after, to be with other humans who could be so real. One older woman had a daughter who was murdered seven years before and the Café was one of the only places she could talk about death. It was to document her healing journey as she forgave the man who killed her daughter, and she saw him receive parole after doing his time in jail. Life can be such an incredible sharing of deep and real experiences. I yearn for this type of richness in my relationships and find talking about the weather not interesting at all.

Several years ago, while I was living in Mexico, Bryan, my first husband and father of my three children died at home. My daughter lived nearby and it was terribly difficult for her. My eldest son called me on Skype to let me know. Bryan had not been well for many years, and he had been housebound on oxygen and many medications for diabetes and heart issues. I was surprised at the depth of my emotion. Though divorced for more than 20 years, of course we had shared many wonderful memories, and we had great love for each other, which sustained our marriage for many years. However, our strained relationship near the end made family weddings and the graduation of our two younger children a challenge.

Deeply feeling his death, I attended our regular morning meditation at The Sanctuary. The others living at the center gave me time and space to speak about it. Then I attended morning yoga. At the end of the yoga class, Christina, our teacher, did something different; she led us through a guided visualization. As we all relaxed in Shavasana, I was walking in a meadow where I sat down on a big stone. Christina said to be open to a message from someone who wanted to talk to us. Bryan came walking toward me. He was young, handsome, and sassy like he was when we first met. He said, "We fulfilled our contract and did what we had to do. No hard feelings." With those words, the tears sprung from my eyes and the grief drained from my body. This reconciliation was a great gift. Christina asked me after class about my experience. When I told her, she said she had a feeling when she saw the huge smile on my face.

He has come a few times since. The next time, I was with my youngest son and his wife in Guatemala. We were out walking when my son's phone began to ring; it was an old reminder he had set to call his dad. At that moment, a tuk tuk chugged past. The drivers usually had their name or a saying written on their canopies. This one had one word: Bryan. We all got it. My son said hello to his dad and we all laughed. It seemed Bryan was able to tap into where we were and take a little trip himself and he showed up at the most interesting times.

At that moment I was feeling so grateful to be alive. I have told my family that I am traveling, exploring the world, and I go wherever my inspiration takes me. I want to live large, and when I die I don't want them to weep for me or wish I had stayed safely at home. I am living life the way I choose, and I want them to be happy for me. I have had a rich and full life. I do believe there is a time for us all to leave and that dying is not a punishment but a soul contract fulfilled.

Another potent visit from Bryan in Guatemala came when I was at a Kirtan, the yoga of sound, or devotional chanting. I enjoyed Paul, Thomas, and the other musicians for their amazing talent. I had taken some magic mushrooms steeped in cacao, to allow myself to be as open as possible. During the event, people lie down to be comfortable, sit up and chant, or dance to express their feelings.

Resting on my mat, I heard Bryan's voice. "I got to go, but you had to stay." What? I had to stay? "Yes and there are some things you agreed to do." What, you left me, I said? He replied, "No, you left me!"(I left our marriage.) No, you left me!"(He left when he died.) I heard a great cosmic laugh as I realized we come and go and leave and love each other and it just circles around endlessly. The universe gave a second deep belly laugh radiating out into the cosmos, and we were floating like little children, skydivers, out in the stars and infinite light.

My friend Joyce is a keen healthy woman in her late 70s. She has a wonderful sense of humor and always loves to learn. In her years, she has seen many loved ones make their transitions beyond this life, including her twin sister and husband of 50 years. Speaking with a friend, Joyce mentioned her intention to die healthy.

Her friend said, "How can you do that? How can you die if you're not sick? No, you get old and more senile and sick and then you die."

"Well I am going to be healthy and just say bye bye when it's time to go," Joyce replied. She has witnessed this with other family members who have passed on. I fully agree.

The great thing about death is that you do it on your own. Finally, you get to do something completely on your own.

~ Byron Katie

I have loved plants my whole life. From the veggies, greens, and herbs I grew for food in the gardens, to the plants I use for health and healing harvested by others, often weeds in the wild. Plant medicine has been a big part of my life to care for my body. But 15 years ago I heard stories of people having dramatic experiences in the Amazon jungle with an ancient plant called Ayahuasca; I was afraid of its power. It is called the Vine of Death and also The Vine of the Soul.

So when it began calling me, I just observed it. Then ten years ago, in the midst of a large Canadian city, the time was right. There was a diet to observe the week before and clear intentions were set. The shaman was from Cusco in Peru and was traveling with his wife and young son. It was an incredible and beautiful experience where I saw colorful mandalas, and truly met my intention of knowing what it's like to live with an open heart. I felt like I was in heaven with the live music and angelic singing in the midst of a group of 40 participants.

After that experience, I was not called again until a couple of years ago. When the plant calls, I know it. I can ignore it for awhile, but I get the message. It was a much more intimate setting with only a dozen people in a large yurt. Once again a diet and intention was an integral part of setting the tone for a good experience. This time it was completely different.

Purging is usually part of the healing and each person is given their own bucket. During my first ceremony I hardly used mine. But during the second one, it became my intimate friend. The medicine went so deep that I entered into a place of shedding. Old patterns and beliefs crumbled like the matrix, dissolving everything between me and what appeared as a window of light. I was guided from within that to know death, I had to be willing to go to the end point of life. I stopped breathing several times. To me it felt like a long pause between breaths, but apparently it was much longer. I heard my name being called, but to reach that window, I could not respond. I remembered from my hospice training that one's body releases all fluids at the point of death.

I made it all the way to that gentle window of light, a very peaceful place. It was the point where one breath would keep me in this life. No breath and I would die. I breathed. Right away, the group of helpers got me up and out of the room. I was a mess and had to strip completely naked in the chilly Canadian November night. The helpers hosed me down and brought warm towels and blankets. I felt like a newborn baby, and in a sense I was. I felt ashamed to put the helpers through such a shitty job. The woman who sat with me said, "You don't understand. It's an honor. To help someone willing to let go of that much, benefits us all. I am grateful to be here."

What an incredible experience. I did not even know that was possible. From the outside of the yurt, swaddled in warm blankets and clean clothes, the purging of others took on the melodic notes of beautiful songs of freedom. Purging is one way to release what we no longer need. The beautiful plant medicine takes us to places inside where we can let go of our pain, sorrow, and sickness. I am very grateful for this knowing of death.

Valuing your life kills you. Valuing your death makes you come alive!

~ Bentinho Massaro

TEN

Choosing Upgrades

You are a living genius. Every human being is born a genius. I am not just saying you have the capacity to be a genius, but that you are one, right now. Your higher purpose in life is to share your particular genius with the world. But what is genius? Today when we think of genius we generally think of it as intellectual prowess, as for example in the case of Einstein.

I would like you to understand genius in a new way. To begin with, you don't have to be intellectual to be a genius. Genius describes you living at your zenith. It is you living your life without holding anything back, owning and therefore transcending your fears. To be a genius is to have the courage to live life with an open heart, as a deep romance. Your genius simply makes you a truly joyous human being. That is your higher purpose—to be radiant for no reason other than being alive.

~ *Gene Keys, Unlocking the Higher Purpose Hidden in your DNA* by Richard Rudd

Upgrades have been magnetized into my life through my passion for living vibrantly. Upgrades create profound miracles shifting us into even more rapid evolution. Exciting as it can be, drawing on our like-minded community for mutual support makes progress more fun and sustainable. And if we don't have a community, we can create it. Even though I travel, I find or create them wherever I go.

I have read countless books and completed so many courses in personal growth and healing over the last 30 years, so I am very selective. My youngest son and his wife's description of the Gene Keys grabbed my attention, even though I was skeptical.

"This is some of the most fantastic information *ever* to come our way," they announced. Upon that decree, I had to check it out and now I agree.

I went online to download my free hologenetic profile, created from my date and place (and time) of birth. We each have a unique profile with eleven keys out of the possible sixty-four. This is the starting point for understanding. It is not fixed like an astrological reading, for our profile evolves as we do. Based on the centuries old Chinese system of divination, the I Ching, we all have sixty-four but our date of birth shows the ones we are here to work more closely with.

Even though Gene Keys is new to me, I passionately share good things with friends and family. I seemed to have a natural capacity to navigate, help, and inspire others confused about how to dive in. The book looks huge and intimidating, but it is *not* meant to be read cover to cover. You must have either the print book or the e-book to move forward into your greatest possibilities.

The journey begins as you read about the first four spheres in your profile. Simply reading the description mysteriously acts on latent codes in our DNA just waiting to be unlocked. I have seen many powerful emotional reactions as others explore their eleven keys.

My friend Joanna was visiting from the UK; we saw that our first four keys were the same. Our birthdays are both in May and two days apart. The other spheres in our profiles were all different. We took turns reading our four keys over a period of several days, and could both feel the power of what was written. We had to pause often, just to take it in. I could feel tingling in my body. The first night I experienced a life review, like an epiphany, as I saw my soul's choice with new eyes. From my childhood until present day, I can see how the events fit. Instead of random experiences I see perfection. This has created a permanent shift in my confidence and a new trust in my path.

I offer these steps for extra clarification. Go to the website (www.genekeys.com) and click on "New to the Gene Keys" link at the bottom of the page. When that page opens, you'll see a tab at the top called "Free Profile" where you can fill out your particulars and download your color profile. Invest in the book; read all four parts of the introduction as they explain so much; read your first four spheres named 1) Life's work, 2) Evolution, 3) Radiance, 4) Purpose. Take time to contemplate these first four spheres as you go. There is no rush. These four are called the Activation Sequence and Richard Rudd suggests you take a year to complete all three steps in the Golden Path.

I took a couple of months to educate myself as much as I could with Richard Rudd's webinars and free resources. You will find them on the Gene Keys website and also on YouTube. When I felt ready, I purchased the Activation Sequence, part one of the Golden Path. I have learned so much by sharing with others, getting them started by sitting with them and reading the first four spheres of their profile together. It is so much fun to see others connect with the wisdom in their own keys.

From the Foreword by Richard Rudd:

> *Welcome to the Gene Keys. This book is an invitation to begin a new journey in your life. Regardless of outer circumstances, every single human being has something beautiful hidden inside them. The sole purpose of the Gene Keys is to bring that beauty forth—to unveil your incandescence, the eternal spark of genius that sets you apart from everyone else. You alone are the architect of*

your evolution.

Each of the 64 keys have a Shadow, a Gift and a Siddhi. All 64 keys have an audio version as well as the written one and some are free, as is forty-nine. I listened to it in the resources and saw it was one of my spheres. The Shadow of forty-nine is called *Reaction*. The Shadow is the way we act without awareness. The Gift is *Revolution* and the Siddhi is *Rebirth*. Once defined, our shadow patterns can be clearly seen and then shifted with our awareness. We can simply take a pause, take a breath, and make a different choice.

Joanna teased me after listening to the audio of the forty-ninth key. In her forthright manner she reminded me of a couple of occasions when that old reaction pattern emerged as we were traveling together. When it does, things never turn out well. So I decided to heighten my awareness and explore what happens with my reactions.

The first time I did not catch myself when I reacted to a whiny child. But I was aware and that is the first step. I was staying in a guesthouse and went into the kitchen early to make myself a hot cup of tea. The place was chaotic with several others taking care of their own needs. I began to react and caught myself. Taking a deep breath I realized I did not have the right to expect a clean empty kitchen since several others lived there. As I paused and relaxed, the space emptied within one minute and I was able to peacefully make my tea.

I decided to create my own boot camp to try it out in a bigger way. I wanted to practice in situations where I had experienced my biggest conflicts. I made arrangements to stay for several days with people I found challenging, as they have a very different worldview. My aim is to create peace in all areas of my life. I learned so much, for I have been conditioned to respond, comment, or defend. I found a response is often unnecessary. But deep listening with an open heart and no reaction can open up miracles. A couple of times I felt stressed and allowed an old reaction to emerge which never turns out well. But no reaction, no judging, conscious listening, and accepting, changed my life in a short time. Thank you Richard Rudd for making this simple and achievable set of programs available.

Ageless Body, Timeless Mind

First published in 1993, the majority of Dr. Chopra's wisdom is still unknown by mass consciousness. Reviewing it helped me understand it on another level and I enjoyed that so much. When we need help to see ourselves as one with the quantum field with all life, Deepak is brilliant. His teachings have been fundamental to the evolution of life and consciousness on our planet.

When I first found his teachings, I wore the cassettes out. I enjoy listening to his voice as he reads his books and to his talks available online. I realized that being open and questioning the "hypnosis of social conditioning" that began in my 40s has created a different set of options in life. It's great to shift the paradigms we are caught in about the topic of aging, and it's best to begin to reprogram ourselves when we are younger.

In the program Dr. Chopra states, "The mind influences every cell of the body. And nothing holds more power over the body than beliefs held in the mind. We can currently rewrite the program of sickness and aging that currently exists in our cells."

His research shows that every year 98 percent of the old atoms in our bodies are exchanged for new ones. Our skin replaces itself every month; our stomach lining is new every five days; our skeleton is new every three months.

There is still an old paradigm that says it takes seven years for our body to regenerate. So it takes some time, contemplation, and desire to be open to radically wonderful information and begin to work with it.

He also states, "If you want to change your body, change your awareness first."

In light of that, let's shift our awareness. Embracing and being open to new experiences and new information instead of being locked in our old comfort zones is one way. Deepak has written a long list books, reads his own audios, and he is featured in countless interviews. His research into the benefits of meditation is an ongoing valuable resource.

Link: www.deepakchopra.com

The Biology of Belief

Dr. Bruce Lipton has been a tireless pioneer. Yet his wisdom about our genes goes unnoticed by mainstream thinking and media, even though he is a well-respected scientist. He has been sharing his findings since the late 1980s and still the hypnosis of social conditioning says that we are victims of our genes.

Dr. Lipton now states that ninety percent of illness and disease is caused by stress. Chronic stress makes the growth in cells shut down. Thus nutrients and blood flow to cells slow or stop when under stress. Stress, especially chronic stress, can simply be a daily worry about life, paying our bills, and doing all the little things we need to do. We often have no idea we are in the midst of chronic stress, for it gets to be the norm. It all connects to our emotions and attitude to life.

Recently Dr. Lipton stated, "One percent of illness is directly related to our genes. The other 99 percent is the way we are living our lives." Why is this phenomenal information being blocked or simply not reaching the general population? How often do you hear or see this old way of thinking? It's time to shift.

Lipton's three books are *The Biology of Belief*, *Spontaneous Evolution*, and *The Honeymoon Effect.* He also has many talks on YouTube.

Link: www.brucelipton.com

Vision for Life

I have known all my adult life that our eyes need the natural light and the reflection of the sun's light is essential to our health. I read *Health and Light* by John Ott when my children were toddlers, so I rarely ever wore sunglasses. Perhaps on a boat on the ocean when the sun is very intense, but otherwise I know my eyes have their own built in shades. I never needed prescription glasses. I openly refused to buy into the idea that our eyes get weaker as we get older. What an epidemic. Years ago my dentist announced that since he was now 40, he had his readers. Really I asked him?. What happens at 40? Why do you believe our eyes cannot continue to function well as long as we live? Why can other parts of our bodies heal and get stronger but not our eyes?

It is a very powerful program in our society that we see better with glasses. It is a fashion statement of a scholar, and sunglasses especially are seen as cool. Celebrities wear them; we should too if we want to be seen as cool and in style. When I see them on babies and young children, I see how thoroughly this paradigm about our eyes has been accepted.

I see wonderfully well, so I have not had my eyes checked. My youngest son, as a teenager, was having trouble seeing the blackboard in school. At his examination, I was aware. The optometrist indicated that he needed a weak prescription now, but that his eyesight would continue to get weaker as he got older. I asked the optometrist about this declaration and by what right did he know what would happen to my son's eyes? He stared at me and was speechless.

"Good one, Mom," my son said when we left. It's one of my gifts to listen closely to what is really being said. Yet, it's difficult to reprogram ourselves beyond these opinions and conclusions. Once the experts give us a diagnosis, it's harder to think for ourselves.

In the late 1990s, I attended weekly events called Synergy Breakfast created by Susan Letourneau in Calgary. Each Friday, mind expanding talks by great speakers were offered with breakfast for a nominal fee.

One such talk was by Dr. Roberto Kaplan, a former optometrist. He offered incredible understandings linking our emotions and deeply held beliefs to the root of eye conditions of every sort. Roberto has a vast array of books and online guided visualizations as well as classes for those who are ready and open to seeing differently.

Link: www.beyond2020vision.com

Enter Meir Schneider. I have known for many years that it is possible to improve our vision. But Meir was born legally blind and taught himself to see.

After reading Meir's book, I made an appointment for the first time in 45 years, to have my eyesight checked. I can still read small and large print but have noticed that my vision is not as clear as it was. I wanted to see what was happening in my eyes that caused the cloudiness so I could understand what parts of Meir's program would be best for me.

The optometrist told me the back of my eye was textbook perfect. I had an astigmatism that caused one eye to see close and one eye to see far. She also found the very beginning of cataracts in my left eye. She said I had unusually small pupils. I told her I was not interested in a prescription but was working on a program to improve my vision. When I left she said to me, "Whatever you are doing, keep doing it. If you need me in the future, you know where to find me."

The programs in Meir's book have the potential to help most every vision issue, from near sightedness and far sightedness to glaucoma and cataracts. It is very thorough and includes the use of medical procedures as sometimes they are necessary. He has a school in San Francisco, presents his wisdom at conferences, sells kits to work with his program at home, and has online webinars.

One of his most potent chapters for me is called the Blind Spots of Conventional Wisdom. In it he details the dangers of sunglasses and corrective lenses and how their use makes our eyes weaker, similar to walking with crutches all day would make our legs weaker. It is amazing food for thought and definitely opens awareness.

Meir states, "There is no help coming from the medical profession to reinforce strength in the eyes. We need to find natural ways to strengthen the eyes so we can see better and depend less on ophthalmology so that it will be less costly to the community. Most people harbor the false belief that their eyes cannot get better. Therefore we need to start with new seeds of hope until more people in the world are willing to work on their eyes. In fact, we need a silent but continuous revolution. To believe in ourselves and in our eyes is to open a window to the heart."

I accompanied my former husband Carl on his journey through cataract surgery. I watched the constant procession of people, like scared sheep, in a fancy facility. Then we went a notch deeper to a specialist. It was creepy for me. The patients all came in wearing heavy black glasses and most had canes or walkers. I made a mental note that I was not taking that path. That was close enough.

Riding in the forest wearing clear glasses a few weeks ago, I had an epiphany. There are a lot of tiny bugs at certain times of the day on that beautiful trail and they seem to get right in the eyes, ears, and mouth if it is open. Suddenly I realized I could have been riding in a cement tunnel or on the freeway in a city. I was completely disconnected with nature and this stunningly beautiful path.

I pulled to the side and stopped. Never having worn glasses, I realized that wearing them while cycling was creating major sensory loss, even though they were clear glass. I removed them and continued to ride. Suddenly I could feel the air, I could smell the trees, I could feel nature all around me through my skin. Wow. Does wearing glasses contribute to our isolation and disconnection on the planet?

Our eyes are said to be the windows to the soul. Who can even say how many ways our eyes connect us to the earth and each other? We have 126 million photoreceptor cells in each retina, with a billion light rays bouncing against some of them every single minute, converting light into visual energy. The possibilities are endless.

Link: www.self-healing.org

The Shadow Effect

Debbie Ford was a wonderful pioneer. With her written work *The Dark Side of the Light Chasers*, online programs, and *The Shadow Effect* movie with Deepak Chopra, she endeavored to model that we all have the same dark side, often called the shadow. Her stunning physical beauty, wealth, and status were a lonely place without meaning and purpose. She shares how perfect her life looked and how empty it really was. Her willingness to be open and transparent about her challenges, recovery from addictions, and acceptance working with her shadow side was profound for me. After watching *The Shadow Effect* movie several times, I wanted to go deeper.

I created space to follow her *21-Day Consciousness Cleanse* less than a year ago. It was the first time in my life that I blocked off a month of time for me. I went to a guesthouse run by Jess, a lovely Mexican woman. I let her know that I would be keeping to myself to work with the program and I took long walks on the beach to process the feelings that emerged. I loved where it took me and am ever grateful to Debbie Ford's courage for it inspired me to also be vulnerable and real. I highly recommend her deeply honest work, which lives on with her books and foundation although she is no longer alive on earth.

Link: www.shadoweffect.com

Lifestyle Medicine

This online program includes movies, interviews, and boot camp programs to open our awareness of our lifestyle choices and take steps to educate ourselves and ultimately improve our lives.

A few important understandings are:

Simple choices every day make a difference; almost any illness can be reversed by lifestyle changes; heart disease, diabetes, rheumatoid arthritis, and high blood pressure are all caused by food choices.

The first step in healing is awareness but creating a healthier lifestyle can be harder if there is no support from your family and your doctor.

We have a powerful ability for self-healing and an amazing capacity to heal and regenerate as we learn to trust our bodies. Dealing with our emotions is vital for ninety percent of all minor scratches and injuries come from unresolved emotional issues. Anger and depression are most strongly linked with heart disease.

Diets high in fruits, vegetables, leafy greens, beans, nuts, and grains are recommended with small amounts of alcohol and meat as more of a garnish than a main meal.

The two best exercises are 20 minutes of walking a few times a week, and lifting heavy weights to exhaustion once a week. The best exercise is the one you do.

The real epidemic is loneliness, isolation, and depression. Antidepressants are the most common drug prescribed. Healthy relationships are essential; having social networks where there is a connection to something larger is essential to health. We must find that connection to God, Universe, Spirit so we know we are not alone and can feel supported.

Link: www.lifestylemedicine.com

To embrace a whole and healthy life, a vibrant life, let's find the joy, create magic, and find ways to laugh often with friends.

Remind each other to relax into expressing more love for life, peacefulness, and gratitude. Creating a whole and healthy life is in our hands. When a part of life is not working to our satisfaction, we are free to choose again.

New possibilities are constantly unfolding on our planet. We cannot even imagine what is possible as our lives are evolving and changing in every moment. The shifts can happen in the twinkling of an eye, especially with our open minds.

ELEVEN

Choosing Unity

Once upon a time, there was a Chinese farmer who lost a horse. It ran away. All the neighbors came 'round that evening and said, "That's too bad." And the famer said, "Maybe."

The next day, the horse came back and brought seven wild horses with it. And all the neighbors came around and said, "That's great, isn't it?" And the farmer said, "Maybe."

The next day the farmer's son was riding one of the wild horses, trying to tame it, fell off and broke his leg. All the neighbors came 'round that evening and said, "That's too bad." And the farmer said, "Maybe."

The next day the conscription officers came around looking for young men for the army and they rejected the farmer's son because of his broken leg.

This simple teaching with story based on Lao Tzu's writings encourage us to open our perception of what is an advantage or a disadvantage. The synchronicity of nature is complex and in the moment we cannot know the final outcome. We cannot imagine what can be the outcome of misfortune, and conversely we cannot know what will be the eventual outcome of what seems to be good fortune.

I learned a wealth of lessons living in Mexico in the winter of 2013. Taking over the kitchen and beginning a huge sorting and cleaning project revealed evidence of cockroaches. I did not know what to do about it and, as the new person on the scene, I did my best to keep on cleaning and put it out of my mind, except when I saw one. The experience evoked a lot of fear in me as I could sense how powerful and intelligent they are. And they move so fast that it made the hairs stand up on the back of my neck.

Finally, Samu, an expressive Peruvian man, put into words

what many of us were feeling. He came down in the dark of the night and switched on a light in the kitchen. To his horror, the space was alive with roaches. His body language and hand gestures were wild as he described their crawling and flying. It would have been humorous if it had not been so terrifying. We all knew that something needed to be done, since the retreat center needed to be clean and safe for residents and guests.

Within a few days a resident met a man whose work was clearing homes of such unwanted invaders. Pete, the owner, was a purist who was against any kind of chemicals being sprayed. We all agreed with that. At the same time, something needed to be done so he agreed to a free assessment, description of the process, and estimated price for the service.

Two men arrived in the morning a few days later. They proceeded to tell us there must be a huge colony under the stove. They wear high rubber boots for protection so the roaches, as they try to escape, cannot run up their pant legs. It was quite descriptive which freaked out some of the group.

At that moment, Gwen, a woman born in Canada who had lived in Mexico for more than twenty years, showed up at the door. "What are you doing?" she demanded. She had seen the truck outside. "Don't do it," she said. "If you kill the roaches, you will mess up some other part of a healthy eco system."

"You people talk of love and light and even named the cat Peace. It seems this does not include insects. Get used to the idea that they are part of life here. There is no cold winter to naturally reduce their numbers. If you truly want the world to be a peaceful and loving place for all, then include the insect kingdom." Bless you Gwen. Her candid words and beautiful insight changed the course of events and affected me deeply. We sat in the yard and talked about unity and accepting all life and tried to figure out another way.

Could there be information online for natural ways to reduce their numbers? Was it possible to create a less than ideal environment? I knew, from my previous work with critters, that we can speak with them and share our intent. A beautiful book called *Kinship with All Life* by J. Allen Boone came to mind. Boone wrote about shifting many things in his life, including an ant infestation. His desire and dedication to respect all life and live in unity and harmony worked. The ants left his space and went to their own anthill where they could live undisturbed. He offered that to them and mentally showed them a can of pest spray that he would use if necessary.

In the Western world there is a belief that cockroaches are filthy. But Pete had researched it and someone had done their PhD project studying them. He showed that they are ancient, extremely intelligent, and clean, but they are big. They have so many legs that allow them to move quickly and catch a person off guard, which can be scary. They thrive where there is clutter and disorganization in cupboards where they can hide and reproduce. In essence they come to help us clean up our act. So we continued to do what we could and also hired cleaning help to do a thorough job.

There are five main steps to reduce their numbers by natural means, making the space less inviting. Besides thoroughly cleaning all areas, access to water must stop. They need water daily but can survive a long time without food. Simple powder available at the hardware store will kill them if they walk through it and it also affects the young ones as they take it back to their nest. I announced to them that they must leave. There was space for them outside but they were no longer welcome in the house. The powder was left out and I told them it was lethal as I respectfully asked them to leave.

It did require consistent mindfulness. Dish draining racks had to be dried off and guests had to be conscious of leaving glasses of water out. House rules were changed to make it undesirable for the critters. Numbers systematically decreased as we cleaned up. The powder did kill some. I cannot say that was the end of them, but it was no longer a pressing issue.

Insects are essential for our survival as humans on earth. If they disappeared, it's said that humans would only last a short time. They perform enormous tasks for us. If humans were not here, life would go on and the planet would thrive. But humans are meant to be here.

We all came here to take this planet of ours to a whole new level of consciousness. We are all meant to be here for this time or our souls would not have brought us here. There are no accidents. Nothing is random. When we choose to see the perfection in all things, we open to a new awareness of unity. When we see our bodies as a whole magical vehicle for our journey, we can begin to relax into the knowing that we are a part of something so much larger than ourselves. The synchronistic whole is right here for us to live into with our awareness.

We are born into a world of duality. Light and dark. Good and bad. Fast and slow. Creating balance and harmony in this sea of choices is an ongoing, moment-by-moment journey through life. We go off in one direction, which is not wrong. Then we go in another direction. Each aspect of life that we explore enriches our experience and we eventually come to a place of surrender to God, Universe, the Divine, Great Spirit, or a greater power with which we are an integral part. The following words are a song that became a favorite at our drumming circles and in our home. We would sing it anytime for emphasis and a good laugh.

Let Life Move Me

Gonna let life move me, gonna let life stir me deep
Gonna let life wake me, from an ancient sleep
Gonna laugh all my laughter, gonna cry all my tears
Gonna love the rain just as deeply as the sun when it clears

Life is the great teacher for all of us. We can open our awareness to glean the messages in every moment. License plates and other signs show up with hilarious confirmation when we choose to see. Animals, birds, and creatures of all types come to offer messages. Learn, seek, and understand. Out of unity comes infinite diversity and abundance.

Life became the great teacher for Carl and I after our head on collision in 2004. We opened to absolute trust and moved to Vancouver Island from Alberta, to have our first winter in a warmer climate. The years 2005 and 2006 were monumental in the journey of unity with all life.

When we moved into our new home on just less than one acre of land on the side of a wildlife reserve, it was incredible. The swans made their daily circle late in the afternoon, honking loudly as they came in for a landing. It was a busy airport as they departed early each day. We got a powerful set of binoculars to observe life around us. It was fascinating to see the swans, whose wingspan is one of the largest, as they ran on the water with their webbed feet to get airborne.

Bald eagles were a sight to behold. The ravens and ducks with their loud voices had much to say. Stellar jays sounded like they were scolding us for invading their space. But the biggest lessons began with the snakes.

Serpent

An area in the center of the circular driveway was left in a natural state. There were lots of bushes and trees undisturbed there. One day, climbing two steps up to have a look, I saw colonies of garter snakes all wound together. The open area on top made a perfect spot for sunning on that warm day in January. It was a shock to my system. Adding to that was their speed at slithering to safety after being discovered. After that we named the area The Serpent Circle. Serpent is the keeper of the south direction in medicine wheel training, and also held a center direction in the medicine bundle teachings, I wanted to learn more and make peace with them.

Kinship with All Life tells the story of a woman in her 70s who had a safe reserve for rattlesnakes that were injured or captured for some reason. Two workers wanted to see what she was doing so they observed her through the glass in the door. She kept her distance at first, talking and gently touching the rattler with a long stick with a soft padded end. She kept telling it there was nothing to fear and that it was safe. Her energy was clear and her words were taken as truth. She walked out with the snake around her neck. Such was her strong belief in unity and her love of life in the form of a snake.

Kinship with All Life says that non-natives are the only ones to get snakebites. He says that an indigenous person has the energy of peacefulness and trust as they walk out in the wild. A non-native often has fear and uses bells or other devices with the illusion that they are in danger and that a bell will keep them safe. That fearful energy causes snakes and other creatures to feel threatened and they only attack to protect themselves. He says a native person, upon seeing a snake would say, *Hello little brother;*

blessings on your way, with a live and let live attitude.

One day we began to mow the lawn. It was disturbing as there were snakes we could not see in the deep grass and one or two got caught up in the mower and died. After that, we announced that we were about to mow the grass and gave a visual message for the snakes and other critters to head to safety. No more snakes met their demise with the mower after that.

One day there was a three-feet-long snake lying on top of the grass. It was the biggest by far that I had seen. As I approached, it did not move, which was unusual. Then I discovered that it was simply a fresh snakeskin. A snake sheds its skin as it grows and this is a symbolic message for us to shed our old skin that no longer serves us. It was a beautiful, soft, perfect skin. As they shed it, they burst out of the head; with the exception of the opening there, it was in perfect serpent shape. What an incredible gift. I will be forever grateful to the snakes on the island for the connection and all I learned.

The whole of our planet is made up of humans of many colors who look, act, eat, and dress in different ways. The customs, languages, and beliefs are more expansive than we can even know. Yet it is perfect. We may not understand, with our human minds, why certain animals or birds are here. We may curse certain insects like flies, mosquitoes, or wasps, but they are part of the whole. There is a need for all in the flow and perfection of the life cycle. We must trust and refuse to kill some of the parts even if we do not understand.

Spider

Returning from several days away, I rushed in to use the half bath. Approaching the sink to wash my hands, a spider so huge, black, and hairy it made me gulp was against the stark white sink. Oh boy. What shall I do? I got a wide mouth glass from the kitchen and a piece of mail. An envelope is the perfect size and stiffness to slide under the opening. I approached the sink and it disappeared down the drain. Whew. Then I relaxed and spoke to it. I showed it in my mind's eye that it could go up into the glass. I assured it that it was safe and I would put it outside.

It was all I could do to allow that huge spider to crawl up inside the clear glass as I held it over the drain in the sink. Slowly I moved the envelope over the opening in the glass. Then I was able to pick it up, tucked in the glass, and make my way outside to let it go. In the 10 years since then, I have had the experience many times, but that first one was monumental. There are so many spiders on the West Coast that it's vital to make peace with them. They have a right to live as much as anything.

A message from spider is to be aware of the webs we are weaving in our lives. Our reality is our own creation. They portray strong feminine energy and remind us to examine how we are using or avoiding our creativity.

Hummingbird

We happily purchased a bright red feeder for hummingbirds. It was so enjoyable to watch their swift humming movement in any direction. Their tiny bodies and wings with such beauty and power are awe inspiring. Hummingbird also holds the north direction in the medicine wheel teachings. One of her messages is to drink deeply from the joyfulness of life and she also brings our ancestors.

Hung by our deck and eating area, the feeder was full of activity. The chance to observe the hummers coming to drink in mid air or perching with their tiny feet brings joy. I never got tired of it. We named one territorial bird *The Bomber*. He would sit in an evergreen tree across from the feeder and swoop in to chase away any other hummingbirds that came to drink. It was fun to watch the antics as a group outsmarted him. One would fly in and he would give chase. Once he was gone a whole group came to drink their fill while he was off chasing the decoy. It seemed they just love to play.

One or two species stay on the island over the winter. But the ones who make the long journey south leave in late August or early September. The males with their bright colors leave first. The females in more subtle shades of green and brown with their young, leave later. One August, we counted forty birds sitting on our clothesline, taking turns at the feeder. They were topping up, two at each spout like a double decker bus, drinking their fill. It was incredible to watch.

Earlier in the summer, one got trapped behind a clear glass panel on the deck. It was buzzing around up and down, like a fly in a window with no escape. We watched in desperation as it seemed exhausted. I went slowly and quietly out on the deck to try to help. I knelt down and put my hand under the area where the hummer was trapped with the idea that I could gently move my hand upward and help her move up to freedom.

To my utter amazement, she flopped back into my hand. Did she have a heart attack? Did the shock kill her? Her feathers felt like velvet. Stunned to find myself holding such a sacred bird, I stood up. As soon as the free moving air hit her, she zoomed off into the trees. But holding her warm velvety body for that precious moment is a beautiful memory.

Bees

For thirty years, both bees and wasps have been my friends. They are both much needed pollinators. Bees message to me is usually about *Being* instead of *Doing*. Seeing them helps me slow down. The wasps are about checking hidden anger. So if they start to build a nest, I look deeper at life. When wasps come during a meal, I simply tell them that there is nothing for them yet and that I will leave something for them later. And I do. I never bat at them or try to swoosh them away and encourage others to tell them no and let them be. Of course they can smell our food and come to investigate.

I have been able to let bees crawl on my clothes and sometimes my bare skin. They love to taste our skin, as do wasps. When our energy is calm, it's safe to let them. But we must know our own energy. I love to see bees disappear into certain flower blossoms. The petals rock and roll as the bee takes a pollen shower. Observing the critters as they intimately connect with the stamen and petals is a sweet sensuous moment.

This year, the hummingbirds seemed to stop coming about mid August and the feeder instead was full of bees. I love bees but that feeder was for the hummingbirds. The number of bees in the backyard increased, and at times the whole feeder was alive with buzzing bees. One day I got it. If the bees needed the nourishment right now instead of the hummingbirds, what difference should that make to me? Why not feed the bees that do so much for us?

Nature is the great teacher and there is always something to learn. When we come to understand the perfection of our journey through life and all we experience, it takes our understanding of unity to whole new levels or depths inside us.

Choosing Unity

How can we look at all of life through the eyes of unity? A vibrant life is for humans and all of life. Whole health means health of the body, mind, spirit, and emotions. To be truly vibrantly healthy, means recognizing that our whole body matters.

Expanding our focus we see that the health of all animals, birds, fish, and insects is intricately woven together with humans. We all need each other. We need the plants that nourish us. We might survive but will never thrive without considering the health of the whole.

The much larger picture is beyond human health. We are part of a family, neighborhood, community, town, province, and country, expanding and including our whole world, without borders. When we see our world from an airplane window, we see it whole and undivided as it really is.

We are part of so much more, as our earth is a speck in the galaxy of many galaxies that make up the universe. And many universes that make up the whole. We are part of so much more. Our planet has been here for billions of years and we are each one speck.

We have come here as one speck or one drop in the mandala of all life that creates the perfect pattern here on earth. We have come here to play our note or sing our song in the infinite notes and songs in the symphony of life. Our note may be huge, or it may be a very short and small one. Unity and the health of the whole depend on all our notes.

No one is an island. We all matter. And as Elders, let's choose again with actions to create the world we know is possible. Let's honor ourselves in our Elder years and what we can offer. Let's work together to create healthy communities wherever we live in the world. It is time for Elders to stand tall, trust our truth, our wisdom, and our intuition. Life is a game and the Universe is always *For Us*.

> *Life is fluid, ever evolving. The more dynamic you are, the more happens in your life, all the time.*
>
> ~ Sadhguru

ABOUT THE AUTHOR

Cori has been a seeker of truth for most of her life. She became passionate to learn about living a vibrant, healthy life when she embarked on the path of becoming a mother. Already interested in eating well, motherhood inspired her to study voraciously to do her best to bring a healthy child into the world. That passion grew even stronger over the years, becoming a guiding theme for her life.

Her deep nature and love of learning has stayed strong. She studied NLP for several years and worked with clients to help them move beyond old unhealthy beliefs and habits. Her desire for a holistic perspective expanded her studies to Reiki, energy healing, and other mind-body techniques. The wisdom of indigenous people took her on a path of shamanic studies, which connected her in a new way to the deeply sacred nature of all life. Her first book *Vision Quest, A Spiritual Awakening*, is an intimate journey with her as she spent two days and nights alone on a mountain, with water but no food or tent, to fully experience the Divine.

Cori loves to travel, lead drumming circles, sacred ceremonies, and workshops on simple steps to embrace our best health. Her passion for living a vibrant life has made her a magnet drawing in a wealth of inspiring tips to claim a juicy life, whatever age we are. She believes that life is meant to be shared in cooperation, and she looks for unity and win-win scenarios.

She loves to inspire others to stand tall and claim the immense power we all have to create a peaceful world where all can thrive.

Beautiful British Columbia, Canada is her home in summer and she finds adventure wherever the warm wind blows her at other times of the year.

You can heal your life
615.851 - Louise Hay
Thank you power,
179.9 - Deborah Norville